EARTH'S AMAZING ANIMALS

NATIONAL WILDLIFE FEDERATION

EARTH'S AMAZING ANIMALS

CONTENTS

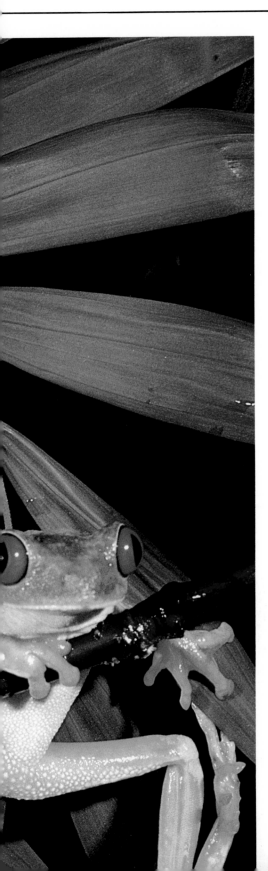

Written by:

THOMAS B. ALLEN
KAREN JENSEN
PHILIP KOPPER

INTRODUCTION

For many years, the National Wildlife Federation's publications have celebrated the wonders of animals and their behavior. We thought it was time to explore the world of animals from a slightly different viewpoint—from within the creatures, if you will. We wanted to know what adaptations enable animals to achieve such feats as seeing in the dark, changing colors in the blink of an eye, thriving in hostile environments where humans would die in minutes, flying backward, diving into water at 60 miles an hour. This was the beginning of *Earth's Amazing Animals*.

Along the way we met many familiar animals, but found in them hidden surprises. The well-known, svelte giraffe, for instance, has a naturally sun-screened tongue with which it plucks thorn-tree leaves under the scorching African sun. Even the lowly flea sports a pair of built-in launching pads so powerful that they can propel the tiny insect 200 times its height into the air. We also discovered a host of little-known creatures: hawks with double-jointed legs; hyraxes, rabbit-sized mammals with suction cups on their feet; tropical fish with switchblades on their sides.

We found sensationalism in nature through record-breakers like the water bears, who have come back to life after 120 years of suspended animation. And we found humor in nature through creatures like the cowboy crab, which fends off enemies with stinging "six-shooters" in its claws. But perhaps most rewarding of all was finding new confirmation of the sense of delicate balance in nature's survival scheme. Take the hunters and the hunted, for one: Each seemingly infallible hunting adaptation in a predator finds its echo in an equally effective defensive adaptation in its prey. Nothing in nature, it seems, happens in a vacuum.

Even after all our years of delving into the lives of animals, we still found plenty of reasons for wide-eyed amazement as we worked on this book. I hope *Earth's Amazing Animals* leaves you with the same sense of wonder about wild things that it gave us as we put it together.

Cecilia I. Parker
Editor

WONDERS IN MOTION

Lightning Legs

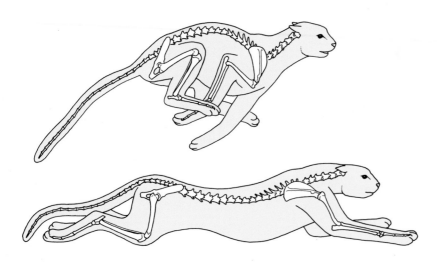

Within the blurred beauty of a cheetah's speed is a secret for running: a flexible spine that the cat bends and stretches to increase its stride as it bounds after prey.

A cheetah crouches in the tall grass of the savannah, body taut, eyes fixed on a herd of gazelles 100 yards away. Suddenly—an explosion of power and speed. The herd instantly scatters, and in that split second the cheetah selects one gazelle for its deadly chase. Hurtling over parched ground in great leaps, the world's fastest land mammal closes on the gazelle in a sprint as fast as 70 miles per hour.

Like a carefully engineered racing car, the cheetah is designed for speed—no holds barred. And although this spotted sprinter may share some speed-giving features with other fast-running mammals—long legs, specially placed muscles, a flexible spine—no other mammal can put 80 feet behind it in one second. The title of "World's Fastest Land Mammal" belongs unquestionably to the cheetah.

One quick glance at a photograph of a standing cheetah is all it takes to be struck by its long, tapering legs. Like other speedsters, the cheetah's lower-leg bones—the shin and the foot—have evolved over eons to be much longer relative to the thigh bone than they are in slower animals. One need only think of a lanky, six-foot athlete eating up the track with his long legs to see the obvious advantage: With long legs, each stride covers more ground.

But a set of long legs is not the only adaptation the cheetah relies on for a longer stride. The cat's shoulder blades are connected to the spine not by a rigid collarbone, as in humans, but by flexible ligaments. The shoulder blades can thus pivot forward with the legs, adding almost five inches to the length of the stride—and helping to keep the cheetah in the fast lane.

Hidden deep within its body lies the cheetah's racing trump card: an amazingly flexible, springing spine that increases the length *and* the speed of the cat's stride.

If we could watch every step a speeding cheetah takes, we would see the accelerating cat pushing off with its hind legs, its sturdy claws spiking the ground for traction. Before the hind legs leave the ground, the cat's spine extends. By adding its thrust to that of the muscular legs, the spine catapults the cat far forward. The more thrust, the greater the distance covered and the greater the speed. As the outstretched front legs hit the ground, the spine springs up, pulling the hips close to the shoulders and whipping the hind legs ahead of the front legs, ready to push again.

But no benefit comes without its price. As any jogger knows, pounding the pavement is a jarring experience. In the cheetah the rough ride is potentially worsened by its springing spine: Each time the spine springs up or down, so goes the cat's body. To overcome the bumpy ride, the cheetah uses its shoulder blades as shock absorbers, slipping them up or down about one inch in the opposite direction of its body. The elegant cheetah races with a smooth ride.

Just as a magnificently designed racing car is useless on the drag strip without a powerful motor, the cheetah's long legs, pivoting shoulder blades, and flexible spine would be useless for overcoming a gazelle without power to set them in motion. In this, too, the cheetah has excelled. As a car has low gears to get it going and high gears to maintain top speeds, the cat has two sets of muscles in its legs: one set for walking and another set for high-speed chases.

The massive high-speed muscles are attached close to the hip joint and, therefore, have little leverage for starting the motion of the leg. They can sustain fast motion, but they can't begin it, just as it is nearly impossible for a person to open a swinging door by pushing near the hinges, but easy for him to keep it swinging that way once a pull at the edge opposite the hinges has started it. In addition, by being placed on the top of the leg, these heavy muscles are away from

the lower leg where their weight would slow the moving foot. The heavy muscles can work hard without swinging very much and can pump the streamlined lower leg easily through the air, speeding the cheetah along.

Paradoxically, the cheetah's speed is both its greatest advantage and its greatest disadvantage when chasing down a gazelle. The cheetah consumes so much energy in its drag-strip acceleration that it cannot continue the race for long. The gazelle has only to zigzag out of the cat's reach for a few seconds. If the cheetah misses in its first explosive attack, it has to stop to rest. In nature, apparently, no adaptation is foolproof. The predator doesn't always catch the prey.

Cheetahs watch for prey with eyes set high on the skull, often spying above the grass while lying low. Large nostrils and lungs give the cheetah the ability to draw in the extra oxygen needed for a fast sprint.

WONDERS IN MOTION

On Helicopter Wings

Give nature an inch and she'll take a mile. One interpretation of fossil evidence suggests, for instance, that a group of ancient reptiles began to glide through the air. In the course of millions of years, their scales became long and flexible, and their bodies lighter with hollow bones and toothless jaws. Their forelimbs, already adapted for gliding, further specialized into wings. Eventually, these reptiles were to become, in a word, birds. But even then the changes did not cease.

Some birds, like loons and cormorants, adapted so well to diving underwater that they could feed exclusively on the deep-swimming fish they caught. Others, like buzzards, took to soaring over land for hours on outstretched wings. Albatrosses became experts at gliding above the seas without touching down for months. Peregrine falcons became earth's fastest organism, diving after prey at better than 175 miles an hour. And some of the very smallest birds, the hummingbirds, became the most versatile fliers of all.

Hummingbirds perform feats that even man's most sophisticated flying machines cannot match. Twisting and turning, they embroider the air with their flight patterns: forward, backward, upside down—even upside down and backward simultaneously. Yet stunt flying is not the only act in the tiny hummers' aerial repertoire. These winged jewels hover in place with such stability that they can insert their long bills into trumpet-shaped flowers and drink nectar as placidly as a southern belle sipping mint juleps through a straw. Further, they can do this whether the flower faces up, down, or waves in the wind.

To understand the hummingbird's remarkable talents, consider the requirements for any object's flight: Airborne machines or animals must be as light as possible, possess a means of rising into the air, and be able to propel themselves forward.

Wings provide lift, or upward movement. Whether a plane's, eagle's, or hummingbird's,

an outstretched wing looks roughly like a teardrop turned on its side: The front is rounded, the top convex, the bottom more or less flat, the back a narrow edge. Air passing over the arched top of the wing travels farther, and therefore faster, than air moving along the flat underside of the wing. The unequal speed of the air results in lower air pressure above the wing than below it. This drop in pressure creates a partial vacuum above the wing, and the high pressure beneath the wing pushes the wing up into the low-pressure area. As the wing rises, so does the bird.

But lift alone does not a flier make. A bird or a plane must have power to move forward. Airplanes need jet engines or propellers in addition to their wings; but, with nature's typical economy, birds derive both lift and power from their wings.

The wing of a bird compares to the hand, forearm, and upper arm in humans. A bird's

A broad-billed hummingbird of America's Southwest (opposite) hovers before a blossom, preparing to sip nectar. The ruby-throated hummingbird of eastern North America (above) readies for take-off. Its legs too weak for hopping, the hummer flies even to change position on a twig.

13

WONDERS IN MOTION

On Helicopter Wings

Ultraflexible shoulder joints give hummingbirds exceptional powers of flight. The illustration below shows how the wings move in forward flight (left), hovering flight (center), and backward flight (right). The rufous-breasted hermit hummer of Trinidad (opposite) lands directly on its eggs without pausing on the rim of the nest.

forearm and upper arm, connected by joints that keep the two parts from twisting while the wing flaps, bear the dense mat of secondary feathers that provide the large surface area so necessary for lift. The hand bears the long primary feathers that pull the bird forward. Spread apart on the upstroke, they create little resistance to the air; closed into paddles on the downstroke, they provide propulsion. During flight, the upper arm and forearm move but little; the hands do most of the work.

A hummingbird's wings may look like the wings of other birds—but there is a hidden critical difference. In seeming contradiction, a hummer's wings are both more rigid and more flexible than its relatives' wings. The rigidity comes from the wing being almost all hand; the forearm and upper arm are extremely short. Further, the joints in the hummingbird's hands are practically rigid, making the wings function more like airplane propellers than they do in other birds. The flexibility comes from a shoulder joint that enables the wing to move freely in almost any direction.

And that's the secret of the hummer's ability to hover. When hovering, the hummingbird beats its wings not up and down diagonally, as in forward flight, but forward and backward in a horizontal figure 8. At the end of the forward stroke, the wing pivots at the shoulder so that the front of the wing still cuts the air to provide lift on the backstroke. Both strokes provide lift, but the propulsion created by the forward stroke cancels the propulsion created by the backward stroke. The hummingbird hovers in a stationary whirr.

Such extraordinary flexibility in wing movement has exacted its price. Hummers cannot soar or glide; they must flap their wings incessantly. Whereas the flight muscles of other birds constitute only 15 to 20 percent of the body weight, they make up about 30 percent of the hummingbird's weight. Such large muscles burn lots of energy.

To support its active lifestyle, a hummingbird will eat half its weight in sugar each day. Yet even that much is not enough to sustain it through cold nights. To keep itself warm, and alive, the tiny bird would have to burn more energy than it has stored. So when night falls and the temperature drops, the hummer does something most unbird-like: It enters a state like hibernation in which its body temperature, breathing, and pulse drop so drastically that the hummer is immobilized. And so it is that these tiny birds live a Jekyll and Hyde existence, spending their days as the most active of all birds and cool nights in a deathlike trance.

WONDERS
IN MOTION

Wings Without Muscles

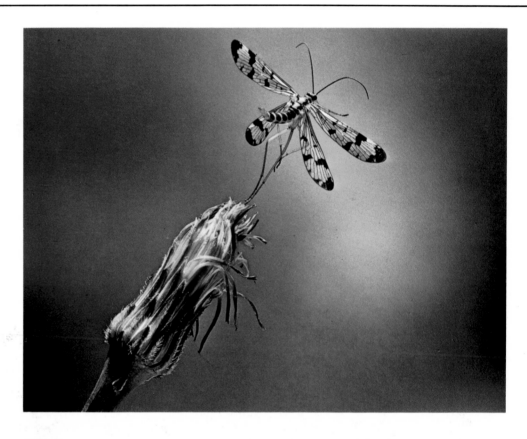

In a burst of energy, a scorpionfly catapults itself into the air to begin its remarkable flight. The flurry of its translucent wings stems from a wizardry of biological mechanics an aerospace engineer would admire.

When man made his first attempts at flight, he imitated the action of the creature whose flight he admired most: the bird. Had he instead marveled at the aerial artistry of the omnipresent fly, his goal might not have eluded him so long.

The common fly is an uncommon flier. The housefly beats its wings 200 times a second. Smaller flies reach the almost unimaginable rate of 1,000 times a second. To achieve such extreme speeds, the fly uses an unusual system of automatic muscles and elastic hinges.

Surprisingly, the fly's flight muscles are not connected to the wings as they are in birds and even in grasshoppers and other large insects. Instead, they are connected to the thorax—the middle portion of the fly's body—which is flexible. As the muscles contract and stretch, they vibrate the thorax in and out. The elastic hinges connect the wings to the top of the thorax and flip the wings up and down at the same rate that the thorax vibrates. Because of this arrangement, the flight muscles operate only indirectly. They flap the wings by vibrating the thorax.

Since a fly's wings beat even faster than its nervous system can carry signals to the flight muscles, the fly relies on two sets of "automatic" muscles. These muscles don't require signals from the brain every time they contract as most muscles do. They contract automatically after being stretched to their limit. The trick is that the muscles are arranged so that when one set contracts it stretches the second set to its limit. The second set of muscles then automatically contracts, stretching the first set, and so on. The fly's body is the next best thing to a perpetual motion machine.

There is a catch, of course. Because of the work required to vibrate the thorax, the muscles gradually lose energy and stretch less each time. To refuel the automatic muscles, a special "starter" muscle gives the thorax a hefty tug, stretching one set of muscles to its fullest. That set then contracts, stretching the other set, and the muscles and wings are off and running again on their own for another 10 to 20 strokes before they start to lose their *umph* and need another jolt from the starter muscle.

The fraction of a second that the muscles require to switch from contracting to stretching ought to disrupt the furious rate of the wings. But the fly has that problem all worked out. The muscles pull the thorax only until the wing reaches the midpoint of its flap, then the elastic hinge flips the wing the rest of the way while the muscles switch directions. At 1,000 beats a second, there is not a fraction of an instant to lose.

The fly controls the direction of its flight by changing the position of its wings. It stabilizes its flight by means of two knobbed stalks called *halteres*. They are attached behind its wings and usually vibrate at the same rate as the wings, but are down when the wings are up and vice versa. Sense organs at the base of each haltere register strain when the fly tilts to one side. The fly then rights itself.

The fly's antennae also control flight. The fly uses its antennae as airspeed indicators by measuring how much they are bent by wind rushing past them.

Because the fly travels at such tremendous speeds in relation to its size, it needs fast reflexes. It has them, to a humbling degree: The fly perceives movement ten times faster than man does. If a fly were to watch a motion picture, it would see the blank spaces between the individual frames. This ability gives the fly an edge against predators—and flyswatters.

Alas, this talented aerialist is rarely appreciated for its flight—or anything else. Although the fly could have served as a blueprint for early airplanes, the Wright brothers were more likely to have shooed them than ballyhooed them.

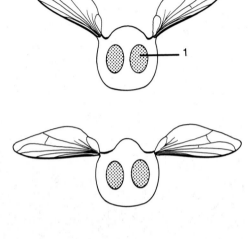

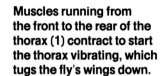

Muscles running from the front to the rear of the thorax (1) contract to start the thorax vibrating, which tugs the fly's wings down.

When the lowering wings reach the midpoint, they automatically snap into the fully lowered position.

The wings are fully lowered and ready for the thorax to change shape and pull them upward.

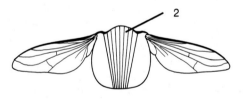

Muscles running from the top to the bottom of the thorax (2) contract to keep the thorax vibrating, and the wings begin to rise.

When the rising wings once again reach the midpoint, they automatically snap into their fully raised position.

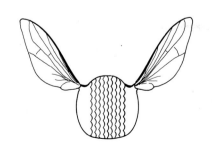

This efficient system permits some flies to beat their wings at the incredible rate of 1,000 times a second.

WONDERS
IN MOTION

Flaps and
Parachutes

Birds fly and bees fly, but rodents, marsupials, lizards, even snakes— can any of them fly, too? Well, sort of. Some of them can glide, a few as far as 1200 feet. Amazingly, these glides are accomplished without any of the special adaptations that give birds flight: hollow bones to reduce weight, feathers to hold air, and wings to slice it.

The crude "wings" of some gliders are flaps of skin stretched between extremities. Other gliders gain some of the effects of wings by flattening their bodies to make them catch air, enabling the creatures to cheat gravity, if only for moments.

Many of the gliders are mammals, and they inhabit many of the forested parts of the world. In the United States, the only ones are the flying squirrels. Large-eyed, nocturnal creatures reminiscent of tree squirrels, they can glide more than 160 feet from tree to tree. The largest glider is the four-foot-long giant flying squirrel of Southeast Asia. Able to glide for up to 1200 feet, the giant flying squirrel even bridges distances between mountain ridges in its forest habitat.

The smallest glider is a marsupial, Australia's tiny feather-tail glider. The diminutive marsupial, whose scientific name aptly translates as "pygmy acrobat," is only three inches long—the size of a small mouse. Its tail, almost as long as its body, is the source of its common name, feather-tail glider. Fringed on each side with hairs that both widen it and give it a flat undersurface, the tail is instrumental in gliding. The acrobat uses it to balance when perched in treetops and as a rudder while airborne.

By spreading its forelegs and hind legs as it leaps, the little acrobat stretches taut the loose flaps of skin along its sides. Like built-in parachutes, they enable the glider to gently ride the air.

Although many times larger than the marsupial, the dramatic flying lemur, a rabbit-sized mammal of Southeast Asia, maneuvers in much the same way on its flights of up to 350 feet. Also called a colugo, it has a

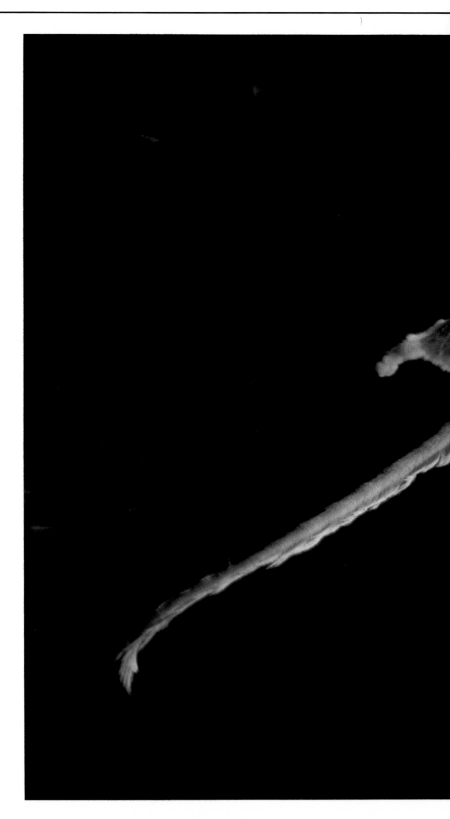

At the end of a glide, a feather-tail glider prepares to land. Its fringed tail, used as a rudder in the air, gives the bright-eyed marsupial its name. Broad, ridged toes give it a sure grip when it alights on its eucalyptus tree home.

WONDERS IN MOTION

Flaps and Parachutes

On flared flaps of loose skin, a flying dragon (right) takes to the air. The large flaps are supported by greatly elongated ribs (below), which the dragon spreads when it glides.

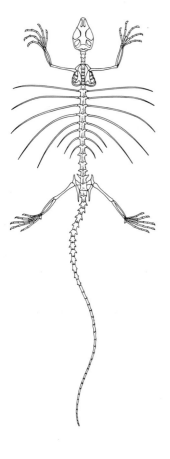

doglike head and a slender, lithe body completely surrounded from the neck to the tail by a sheath of skin resembling a fur cloak. This membrane, which even stretches between the hind legs and the tail, is the largest of any gliding mammal's. When the flying lemur launches itself from a tree, it spreads its limbs, and the gliding membrane billows around it, transforming it into a seemingly weightless spirit of the night.

The flying lemur steers its flight by listing its body from one side to another. As it prepares to land, it lifts its tail. This acts as a brake and raises the front of the body, readying it to grasp its tree-trunk target with needle-sharp claws.

The tropical forests of southeastern Asia are home to yet another remarkable animal, the flying dragon. It is vastly different from the flying lemur, yet has the same ability to take to the air.

The flying dragon, a lizard, is one of a variety of reptiles specially adapted for gliding flight. While reptiles may seem improbable fliers, they were the first vertebrates to develop flight capabilities, millions of years before birds were even on earth. Today's gliding reptiles, however, are not descended from those earliest flying reptiles. Lacking strong chest and shoulder muscles, they are

unable to flap their "wings" like birds; they can only glide. But they do that quite well.

The gliding membranes of the flying dragon are loose folds of skin on its sides that the lizard stiffens for flight by spreading several pairs of greatly elongated ribs. When at rest, the drab gray, brown, and black dragon presses the ribs flat against its body. Its skin flaps fold in such a way as to be scarcely noticeable. But when the animal is in flight, its brightly colored orange-and-black wings make a spectacular sight, earning the dragon lizard the popular name of butterfly lizard.

Another spectacular sight, even without its brilliant hues, is one of the most unusual gliders of all—the paradise tree snake. This slender, three-foot-long snake of the East Indies has several surprising talents. For one, it is an outstanding climber able to slither up tree trunks and even the walls of houses with ease. Furthermore, the paradise tree snake can spring for short distances: By tightly coiling itself and then unwinding rapidly, it flings itself toward its destination.

But more amazing is this wingless, membraneless creature's ability to glide from tree limb down to the ground for distances of up to 100 feet. It takes flight by reshaping its long, rounded body to make it function as much as possible like an airplane wing. When airborne, it holds itself rigidly straight and spreads its many ribs as wide as they will go while sucking in its belly so that its underside is concave. What would have been a dangerous vertical fall becomes a safe diagonal descent. To land, it lifts its head to check the speed of its fall, and gently alights on the ground.

Just as most snakes slither, most frogs jump. But, sure enough, several species have developed the ability to glide. These flying frogs inhabit the same exotic tropical forests as the flying snakes, flying dragons, and flying lemurs. Somber green and brown splotches hide them among the leaves despite their incessant activity, for these robust frogs hunt aggressively. They seek out their insect prey rather than waiting patiently for dinner to come by on the wing.

As part of their refined hunting technique, they stealthily glide 20 to 40 feet from one tree limb to another or to the ground. To accomplish this, the frog arches its back, pulls in its stomach, and spreads its toes wide to stretch the webbing in between. Like the flying dragon, some flying frogs flash colorful patches on their bellies and legs as they take off.

Another animal that has earned its wings is the flying fish. Unlike the flying frog, which glides after prey, the flying fish takes to the air to escape enemies.

For the six- to eighteen-inch-long fish to become airborne, it must first swim very fast—about 15 to 20 miles per hour—just beneath the surface of the water. When it has gathered momentum, it bursts through the surface of the water and immediately extends the long, winglike fins located on its sides just behind its head. It does not flap its "wings."

The flights are short; most flying fish lose airspeed after four to twenty seconds and reenter the water. Some hearty fish, however, can prolong their flights by as much as five times their normal length by dipping their tails in the water and fluttering them furiously to relaunch themselves. The grace of these aquatic fliers makes the figure of speech "a fish out of water" seem most inappropriate.

Beautiful as a jeweled necklace, a paradise tree snake extends its head away from a branch in preparation for its glide down to earth.

WONDERS IN MOTION

Ballast Tanks

Resplendent in its flashy make-up, a clown trigger-fish cruises its home waters. Like most fish, it can remain at a given depth almost effortlessly by using a gas-filled chamber in its heavier-than-water body to match the water's buoyancy.

Anything lighter than water floats. Anything heavier than water sinks. These are simple concepts a child playing near a pond will grasp in minutes.

But how do the creatures in the pond—and in the rest of the earth's waters—reconcile themselves to these facts? For although fish flesh is heavier than water, few fish are limited to life on the floor of the sea. How do they keep from sinking or from expending tremendous amounts of energy to stay afloat, as does the shark? Because the shark has no buoyancy system, it must remain in eternal motion, lest it settle to the bottom of the sea.

A submarine demonstrates a simple solution to the problem: ballast tanks in its hull. When the tanks are filled with water, the submarine descends. When they are filled with air, the submarine rises. In fish, internal chambers called swim bladders work in much the same way. By regulating the amount of gas in its swim bladder, the fish regulates its depth underwater.

Most fish have one of two types of swim bladders. In most fish that live in shallow water or are constantly near the surface, fine tubes connect their swim bladders to their throats. The fish increase their buoyancy by swallowing air when they are at the surface and decrease buoyancy by releasing air through the mouth when they are below the surface.

Fish that inhabit deep water cannot rely on skimming its surface for air. Rather, the fish's bloodstream carries gases to and from the bladder. As the blood passes through a special system of tiny blood vessels next to the swim bladder, gases dissolved in the blood are absorbed into the bladder. The more gas the bladder absorbs, the lighter the fish becomes. The system is so efficient that a fish can dart wherever it pleases, swimming as fast as it wants, while the swim bladder makes constant, finely tuned adjustments at just the right pace.

Even the mightiest of the sea's creatures need help negotiating its depths, for it is the sea itself that is always mightiest of all. One of its giants, the sperm whale, has a buoyancy regulating system whose action was long hidden by the mystery of the animal itself and by the lore of whaling.

Among the riches whalers sought in their catch was the bounty of spermaceti oil that filled cavities inside the sperm whale's massive head. But how the oil served the whale was unknown. One inaccurate assumption lives on in the whale's name: Early whalers thought the oil was the animal's sperm.

A recent investigation has suggested a more plausible function: The spermaceti oil may help the whale regulate its buoyancy. To dive deeply, whales must reduce their buoyancy, and the oil may help them do so by thickening into a solid, waxlike substance as the whale descends into the increasingly colder waters of the deep sea. This solid substance would make the whale's head denser and, thus, the whale less buoyant.

When the animal needs to rise, presumably it shunts its body heat to the store of oil in the head to warm and reliquify the oil, thereby increasing buoyancy.

Two other renowned creatures, both mollusks, have unusual buoyancy systems. The chambered nautilus is famed for its beautiful shell which, when bisected lengthwise, reveals as many as 36 individual chambers. In life, the chambers serve as ballast tanks. They are filled partly with water, partly with air, and are connected by a tube that transports gases. The tube fills the chambers with gases to increase buoyancy and empties them to decrease it.

The cuttlefish is well known for its internal shell. Known as cuttlebone or seabiscuit, the shell is often given to caged birds as a dietary supplement. But in the squidlike cuttlefish, it supports the body and helps it float by trapping gas and fluid in its pores.

The animal's degree of buoyancy depends upon the ratio of gas to fluid. And light influences the ratio. The nocturnal cuttlefish decreases its buoyancy during the day when it is exposed to light and increases buoyancy during the night, when the creature rises — literally — to greet the dark.

The cuttlefish controls its buoyancy by juggling the ratio of gas to fluid in the cavities within its porous, internal shell.

WONDERS IN MOTION

Jet Propulsion

Jet propulsion seemed to be man's marvelous invention when it carried the first jet airplane aloft. But it just mimicked a source of power that several kinds of animals have used for hundreds of millions of years. Jet propulsion may be one of the oldest means of locomotion among complex organisms.

The principle itself is known to any child who has blown up a balloon and let it go: Air within the shrinking balloon escapes, propelling the balloon in the opposite direction. The faster the air escapes, the faster the balloon speeds along. And that, basically, is how jet propulsion works in such ancient animals as jellyfish and in later arrivals like squid, scallops, file shells, and some fish. For them, escaping water works like the escaping air in the child's balloon.

Jet propulsion plays a fairly minor though useful role in the lives of fish like the predatory pike, well-known for its voraciousness. When another fish comes within striking distance, a pike whips into action its large tail and dorsal fin and at the same time contracts its gill chambers. The jetstream of water thrusting toward its tail from its gills increases the speed of attack.

The jet propulsion champions are squids, the original mollusk's most unusual living descendants. Many of their relatives have shells for protection—either single shells as in snails or paired ones as in clams. But the squids disposed of such cumbersome armor eons ago; they found safety in the speed of jet power.

A squid's vital organs lie behind its tentacles and eyes, hidden inside a muscular tube called the mantle. The mantle has an open collar at the bottom near the eyes, and the space between the mantle and the organs is filled with water. At will, the squid closes the collar and contracts the mantle, squeezing the water in the cavity out through a nozzle, the siphon.

A squid can point its siphon up, down, ahead, or sideways, steering its body in the opposite direction, often with amazing

By jetting water out of its siphon—above and left of eye here—a large squid swims at speeds up to 23 m.p.h.

28

The chambered nautilus' shell grows in a coil of connecting chambers with the animal inhabiting only the outermost one. The nautilus adjusts gases in the inner chambers to control buoyancy and rise or sink like a submarine. To swim, it draws in water through a flap near its eye and expels it through the flexible siphon.

speed. Large species may travel faster than 23 miles an hour. Some smaller squids jet-propel themselves fast enough to breach the surface of the water and fly through the air for 50 yards and sometimes reach heights of 20 feet. These "sea arrows," as they are called, sometimes land on ship decks.

The chambered nautilus uses a similar kind of siphon. But because this unusual animal has a hard shell it uses a different method to jet the water. Water enters the mantle cavity through a flap near the eye (see illustration), and the flap closes. Then two powerful muscles attached to the triangular hood and to the sides of the shell near the first, and largest, chamber contract, pulling the body toward the back of the shell. The body fills the cavity, forcing the water to escape past the gills and out through the siphon. Like the squid, the nautilus directs its movement by pointing the siphon away from where it wants to go.

Most shelled mollusks are known for their slow or totally sedentary ways. Wit-

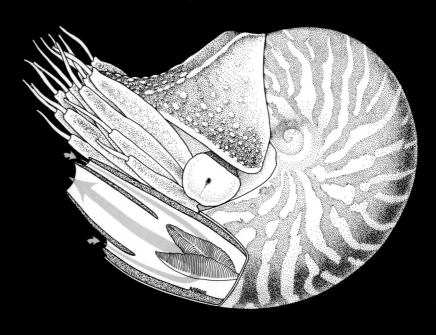

WONDERS IN MOTION

Built-in Highways

A cross spider deftly halts its free fall by pulling the anchored silk thread to one side. The spider ejects its portable pathway as a liquid that quickly hardens into a flexible strand.

Any hiker groping to find his next foothold on a steep, wooded slope has good reason to envy the humble spider and snail. Both spider and snail have built-in transportation systems, natural highways manufactured inside their bodies. The spider, while it can throw all eight legs into motion to walk, has in its silken threads an additional, speedier transportation system that involves a leg or two at most. And with its slimy trail, the snail can glide where hikers fear to tread.

The simplest way for a spider to get down from a high place is to ride its own express elevator. The spider grabs a strand of silk with one of its legs and attaches it to something solid. Safely anchored, the spider either free-falls or lets itself down by pulling out silk gradually. In either case, the spider stops at whatever floor it wants by tugging the silk strand to one side, thus halting the flow of silk from its body.

The silk thread—comparable in strength to nylon thread but far more elastic—is manufactured as a liquid in glands in the spider's abdomen. All spiders have at least three, and some up to seven, different types of silk glands. Each of these glands produces a different type of silk. Spiders use one type to wrap their prey, another to form "attachment discs" that anchor the threads, and yet another to create the sturdy "drag lines" on which they lower themselves. Female spiders also produce a special silk thread for making the egg sac.

Tiny ducts take the liquid silk from the glands to structures on the exterior of the spider's body, the spinnerets. Protruding from the lower abdomen, the spinnerets resemble six tiny fingers. Well-muscled, each one is able to move independently or in coordination with the other spinnerets. When working together, the spinnerets blend silk from the different glands, custom-tailoring their threads for strength and thickness.

Muscular valves near the spinnerets'

A moist, soft-bodied land snail glides easily along a glistening mucous trail, even over rough, dry terrain.

spigotlike openings share a similar function. They determine the diameter of the spigot's opening and, thus, the thickness of the silk thread that passes through it.

As silk emerges from the spigot, an amazing transformation takes place; it changes from a liquid to a solid, yet extremely elastic, thread. The hardening is caused by tension in the silk line, which realigns its molecules.

The silk threads consist mainly of protein, a substance the spider uses very resourcefully. Before building a new web, the spider eats its old web to quickly recycle its proteins.

Speed is necessary in producing new silk, for the spider is a relentless weaver. Unlike the silkworm, which constructs only one silk cocoon in its lifetime, many spiders weave a web a day, and they usually do it in under an hour.

For the land snail and for its close relative the terrestrial slug, on which this method of locomotion was first studied, construction of the highway is an even more constant activity. The snail relies on its slimy pathway to take it everywhere it goes. The roadway consists of two kinds of mucus. One kind, thin and watery, exudes from microscopic glands on the bottom of the snail's large single foot. The other kind, thick and sticky, is manufactured by a single gland at the front of the foot.

The snail presumably varies the proportions of thin and sticky mucus depending on its traveling needs. If it moves uphill and needs more sticking power, the snail uses more of the sticky substance. If it shifts to level ground, it adds more watery mucus.

The snail's foot moves in waves. Sections of it hold fast to the slime while other sections raise off the sticky surface to stretch forward and reanchor themselves. Remaining where it was laid, the slime path glistens like a silvery streak in the sun, the telltale mark of a snail on the move.

Traction for Action

To make a living, most animals must move about. But some have to do it the hard way—by climbing slippery rocks or smooth-barked trees; by leaping from narrow ledge to narrow ledge or walking upside down on ceilings; by walking over ice or scrambling across shifting hot sand; or even by sticking tightly to a fast-paced ride. Whereas humans have invented machines to take them everywhere they want to go, the "inventions" of the traction masters rest in the design of their bodies.

Take tree frogs, for example. Most of them prefer to live in trees, carefully leaping from one branch to another and climbing up trunks in their search for food and shelter. Far too small to wrap their arms and legs around trunks or big branches, these agile frogs must rely on the shape of their bodies and the flattened discs on the ends of their toes and fingers to secure them to their leafy perches.

A rotund terrestrial frog would be hard pressed to stay put on a slender tree limb; like a rubber ball placed on a thin rail, its likely fate would be to roll off and topple to the ground. Not so the dainty tree frog. A tree frog's body is broad and flat, a shape that lets it press proportionately more of its undersurface against a limb than a round terrestrial frog can. Because the tree frog's weight is distributed over a greater surface area, it is much more stable.

The tree frog would need nothing more than stability if it only lounged lazily in tree branches. But tree frogs must eat. To find food they must move—walking up trees, along branches, even on leaves. For getting around on trees, a tree frog uses its pads, expanded discs at the end of each finger and toe. These pads help to increase the frog's overall body surface, but they do much more than that. Bathed in the same secretions that cover the rest of the body, the discs spread this froggy glue with each step. The pads stick to the surface of leaves and bark as the bottom of a wet glass sticks to a table top. And just in case the tree frog

needs additional gripping power, the discs are covered with bristlelike cells that catch on minuscule irregularities in the surface.

Trees are great spots to find insect feasts, and some Southeast Asian island tree frogs sometimes share this bounty with a big-eyed, long-legged, short-bodied mammal, the tarsier. Champion jumper among primates of its size, this four- to six-inch-long nocturnal hunter can leap as high as four feet and masters long jumps of six feet. When it leaps onto a tree branch to nab an insect, the tarsier reaches out its feet for the landing. And landing is easy. Along the en-

Both a big-eyed tarsier (above) and a red-eyed tree frog (opposite) hang on with fingers adapted for arboreal life. The tarsier's long, padded fingers have anti-skid treads. The frog's round, flat fingertips increase the surface area of its grip.

WONDERS
IN MOTION

Traction for Action

A polar bear ranges far across snow and ice fields in search of food, walking on broad feet insulated with hair that provides traction. The bear's front feet are also partially webbed for swimming.

WONDERS IN MOTION

The Launch Pad

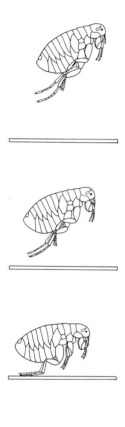

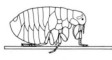

Rubbery pads near its hind legs (see dot in bottom drawing) launch a flea up to its much larger victim. A flea jumps when it senses the smell or warmth of a nearby animal, or detects the carbon monoxide from the prey's breath or the air currents created by the prey's movements.

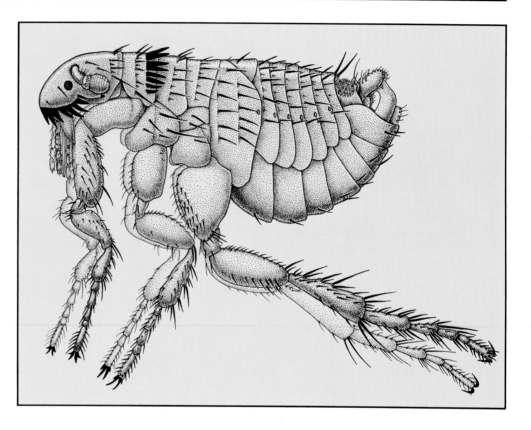

Have you ever left the family dog in a kennel over summer vacation, only to return home to a hotbed of bloodthirsty fleas? They hungrily leap out of the carpet, attacking your ankles and legs. These pesky pogo sticks hurl themselves 12 inches into the air, nearly 200 times their height. How do they do it?

Strong muscles in the hind legs provide part of the answer, but these muscles alone cannot catapult the flea to such heights. The additional power comes from hidden launching pads built into the flea's body.

These launching pads are made from an amazing rubberlike substance called resilin. Like synthetic rubber, resilin springs back to its original shape after being stretched or compressed, releasing stored energy. Yet man's best products pale when pitted against nature's. Resilin releases more energy, bounce for bounce, than any man-made rubber to date. Furthermore, resilin never loses its

spring as man-made rubber eventually does; resilin continues to deliver the same potent power no matter how long it has been distorted or how many times it has been pulled or pushed out of shape.

The flea has two launching pads, one on either side of its abdomen, just above the hind legs. Before leaping, the flea pulls its legs up against its body, putting pressure on the launching pads. Tiny hooks lock the legs in this cocked position; without any further muscular effort, the flea can maintain a steady pressure on the launching pads. Cocked and ready to spring at a moment's notice, the flea can afford to patiently wait for a hapless victim.

When ready to leap, the flea unhooks its legs and presto! The launching pads suddenly snap out to their original shapes, thrusting the legs downward. They strike the ground with a surge of released energy, launching the flea toward its lunch.

Hydraulic Legs

A jumping spider makes its living by pouncing. Inching forward on short, stout legs, it stalks its prey with the stealth of a cat. Suddenly the spider leaps through the air and lands on its insect meal with deadly accuracy.

Yet for all its jumping prowess, this mighty hunter's muscles can only flex its legs. To jump as it does—up to 25 times its own length—the spider relies on a powerful hydraulic system.

As it prepares to pounce upon its meal, the spider fastens a safety line of silk to its takeoff point and folds its legs tight against its body. In less than the blink of an eye, the hydraulic system in the body vigorously pumps blood into the hollow centers of the hind legs. Like a garden hose suddenly made taut by the onrush of water from a just-opened spigot, the spider's legs forcefully straighten. The spider takes off like a silent missile. Insects, beware!

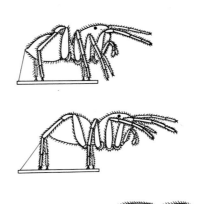

A jumping spider takes the precaution of anchoring a safety thread before takeoff. Lacking muscles to extend its legs, the little leaper relies on a hydraulic system to force-fully straighten its hind legs for a send-off.

WONDERS
IN MOTION

Legless Locomotion

Perhaps "form follows function" in modern architecture, but in nature function and form go hand in hand. Witness snakes: Their singular shape and mysterious movement have been inextricably connected since their lizardlike ancestors first took to burrowing in the earth and, over time, lost their limbs.

A legless animal might seem an evolutionary disaster, a creature unable to move in search of food, a creature incapable of fleeing from a hungry predator. Yet the legless snakes move in wonderful ways. They slither on the ground at speeds up to 15 miles per hour; they climb trees; they skim the surface of unresisting desert sands. In fact, snakes are so successfully mobile that they can choose from four distinct methods of travel, depending on the terrain.

To move without legs, a snake must use its entire body—bones, skin, muscles—as one perfectly coordinated organ of locomotion. The key to its movement rests in the snake's remarkably flexible body.

To keep the long cylindrical shape as flexible as possible, the number of vertebrae has multiplied. Where humans have 32 backbone segments, some species of

snakes house a staggering 400. The more vertebrae, the better the spine can bend.

Snake skin, too, has become specialized for motion. The snake's belly is covered by broad, flat scales called scutes. Overlapping like shingles on a roof with their free edges pointing to the rear, these scales grip the ground, giving the snake traction.

Finally, snakes boast one of the most intricate muscle systems ever concocted by nature to move a body about. One set of muscles, connecting the vertebrae to each other and to the ribs, enables the snake to bend its body in gentle curves or wrap it tightly in coils. Another set, linking scales to ribs and each scale to its neighbors, gives a snake complete control over the movement of each scale on its underside.

For straight-ahead travel, snakes use the rectilinear or caterpillar method. To move, a snake grips the ground with sets of scales at intervals along its belly and pulls itself forward. As the snake moves, new sets of scales grip the ground ahead, while the original sets disengage. By anchoring and lifting its scales, the snake travels in a smooth glide. Ideal for sneaking up to prey, this method is, nonetheless, slow.

A scarlet king snake of the southeastern United States makes its tangled way along a branch. A snake's intricately coordinated bones, muscles, and skin more than compensate for its lack of legs.

For a faster pace, snakes travel by lateral undulation. If you have ever startled a snake in the grass and watched it slither away, chances are it escaped using this method. To move forward, a snake bends its body into a series of S-curves, pushing each bend against any irregularity in the terrain.

But lateral undulation can be used only on rough terrain, and, often enough, snakes must move through smooth-walled rock crevices. Here they rely on the concertina method. The snake wedges a couple of bends near its tail against the crevice wall. Once the rear of its body is firmly anchored, the snake stretches its neck forward as far as it will go. Then, wedging a couple of bends near the front of its body against the walls, the snake pulls its tail forward. Bending and stretching, the snake inches through the length of the crevice. A modified version of this method is used by slender tree snakes for moving from limb to limb. Wrapping its tail around a branch, the tree snake then stretches its body, keeping it as rigid as possible, until its head reaches another branch.

For the difficult task of traveling across hot, shifting sands, some desert snakes use the sidewinding method. To move forward, the snake "winds sideways," in a kind of sinuous leapfrog. Pressing its tail against the sand, the snake arches its body off the ground in a loop and throws its head and neck a little distance forward. As its head touches down, the snake whips the rest of its body out to the side, and then again lifts its head and neck off the sand, ready to fling them forward again. As the snake moves along its invisible path forward, its tracks lie crosswise, like railroad ties, on the sand.

Each method can be broken down on paper, but no description can match the snake's smooth elegance as it combines the steps into a seamless performance more graceful than a carefully choreographed dance. The snake's secret lies in the perfect interaction of its anatomical parts—and in the perfect marriage of form to function.

Legless Locomotion

Snakes move in wonderful ways: A corn snake (opposite) climbs a tree by moving like a living accordion. A North American sidewinder (above) plays serpentine hopscotch in desert sands. The skeleton (left) displays the many-pieced spine that gives snakes their remarkable flexibility—the key to legless locomotion.

2 FEEDING THE BODY

FEEDING THE BODY

Going Fishing

priately, they have waterproof fur and can swim. They both zero in on their potential meals by using their sonar to detect disturbances on the surface of the water. Then they swoop down, raking the surface with the extraordinarily long claws on their hind feet. One of the species even has a built-in creel: cheek pouches the bat can fill before flying off to its roost to dine. Another novel fisherman, the fishing cat of southern Asia, has partially webbed front feet which it uses to scoop fish from streams and estuaries.

All crocodiles and alligators fish for food. The slender-snouted gavial does its fishing underwater. To go under, the gavial seals itself as tight as a submarine on a deep-sea mission. Ears and nostrils clamp shut, and its tongue seals off its throat so the gavial can open its mouth while fishing without flooding its lungs. Once it has submerged, the gavial violently slashes its snout sideways and snaps its jaws. As for the fish, well, the gavial probably has precious few stories about "the one that got away."

Nature's fishermen are a diverse lot: the fishing bat (above) uses sonar to detect ripples on the water's surface, indicating a fish beneath; the fishing cat (right) snares fish with its webbed feet; the gavial's slender snout (opposite) is a perfect tool for underwater fishing.

Underwater Stalker

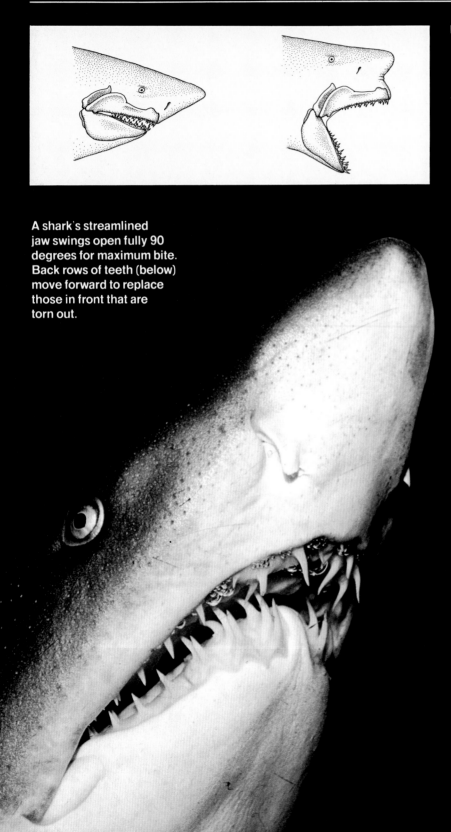

A shark's streamlined jaw swings open fully 90 degrees for maximum bite. Back rows of teeth (below) move forward to replace those in front that are torn out.

The shark's ugly appearance invites people to worsen its already evil reputation as a ravenous instrument of fate. Novelist Peter Benchley called the great white shark in *Jaws* "an angel of death gliding toward an appointment preordained." Underlying such images are awesome truths about the perfection of the shark's adaptations for finding and killing prey. Its reputation as an unerring hunter results from a remarkable array of physiological systems, including the ability to locate prey by means of electricity. Its image as a man-eater is grossly exaggerated, however. Sharks attack about 30 people a year worldwide, fewer than ten fatally.

The mouths of sharks are equipped with a variety of ingenious devices for catching food. While some possess a single row of flat teeth in the upper and lower jaw for grinding, most species have several rows of sharp triangular teeth—smooth-edged for stabbing and grasping, or serrated for ripping into flesh. Some shark's teeth are hinged; when the jaw opens, they swing forward, enabling the shark to get large prey into its mouth. As the jaw closes, the teeth swing back down to grasp the victim firmly while the shark violently shakes or twists to wrench loose a mouthful.

Multiple rows of teeth serve the same purpose as a car's spare tire, and sharks need spares because many of their teeth are torn out during feeding. Unlike most vertebrates' teeth, sharks' teeth are not set in the jaw. They are loosely set in soft gums, one row lying behind the next. When a tooth falls out, one behind it moves forward to take its place. Some sharks lose and replace all the teeth in the first row in as little as eight days—a turnover that continues throughout their lives.

In a sense, sharks are all teeth. Instead of having normal fish scales, shark skin has razor-sharp, toothlike scales called *denticles.* Only the rows of teeth that fill the shark's mouth are more dangerous than the abrasive skin. And it's no wonder

—large, modified denticles are exactly what those teeth are.

The shark's supreme hunting skills result from its extraordinary sensory systems. It finds food by a methodical search pattern involving sound, smell, water pressure, sight, and the prey's own electrical field.

Because sound travels well through water, a shark's ears needn't be highly sophisticated to detect low-pitched, intermittent sounds coming from thousands of yards away. These sounds are the kind made by a struggling fish, and sharks are strongly attracted to them.

If it swims within several hundred yards of a wounded fish, a shark can home in on the smell of the blood in the water. Two-thirds of the shark's brain is devoted to monitoring odors in the water. A shark can detect blood diluted by as much as one part blood to ten million parts water.

A structure called the *lateral line* is useful in detecting prey located within 100 yards of a shark. The lateral line is the thin line visible on the sides of most fish. It comprises small, fluid-filled sacs, each contain-

ing a hairlike device that responds to pressure changes in the water. The lateral line allows fish to feel the movement of distant creatures via the water itself.

At fewer than 50 feet, the shark's eyes come into play. They keenly detect movement even in dim undersea light, and some sharks can also distinguish color. As the shark closes in for the kill, however, opaque inner eyelids draw over each eye to protect them during the imminent struggle. In the final seconds, the shark depends on what is, perhaps, its most remarkable ability: the perception of electrical fields.

Muscle movement generates electrical currents that leak easily through the skins of marine fish. By means of special organs in its snout, a shark can home in on a hidden fish as far away as ten feet.

A new theory holds that sharks are not the sea's most primitive fish but a sister group of the bony fish, an independent evolutionary line. Certainly, the shark's complex sensory systems represent a high degree of adaptation and one of the world's anatomical marvels.

A meal ends a hunt that may have begun thousands of yards away when the shark first heard its prey. At a closer distance, the shark can smell the meal; then it feels its motion with sensory organs that detect variations in water pressure caused by the prey's motion. At close range, the hunter may use its eyes to zero in on its food. Finally, sensors in the shark's snout pick up the prey's electric field.

FEEDING THE BODY

Opening Hard Packages

An assassin bug (above) pierces the hard body of another insect with its needlelike beak and injects a fluid that destroys nerves and dissolves soft tissues. Then it sucks its victim dry. The red crossbill (right) forces apart the scales of evergreen cones with its odd beak. Then it picks out the seeds with its tongue.

Starfish also find bivalves to be choice food, but they assault them in an entirely different way. These spiny-skinned animals of the seafloor move about on hundreds of tiny tube feet on the bottoms of their many arms. These hundreds of individually controlled tube feet also serve as eating utensils. The starfish straddles a clam, oyster, or other bivalve and forces it open by attaching the suction cups on the ends of its feet to the two sides of the shell and tugging away until the bivalve tires. An opening only six-fiftieths of an inch wide is enough because the starfish then sends its own stomach out of its body and between the victim's parted shells. After the stomach has digested the meal, the starfish tucks its belly in and moves on — like a litterbug, leaving only the empty hard package behind.

Assassin bugs, as some 3,000 species distributed over most of the world are known, also digest their food outside their own bodies. These hunters pounce on other insects and grasp them with powerful forelimbs, sometimes equipped with adhesive pads. After a successful catch, the assassin stabs through its victim's hard shell with its needlelike beak and injects a powerful poison that attacks the nerves. One such killer can dispatch prey 400 times its weight in ten seconds. After the poison takes effect, it liquifies the prey's internal tissues, which the little assassin then sucks up, leaving an empty shell.

Far less ferociously, some members of the finch family pry their food from especially tough seed containers. The crossbills of North America sometimes eat insects and hardwood seeds, but their unusual bills are best suited for taking seeds from evergreen cones. These birds are perfectly named, for the upper and lower halves of their bills cross at the tip and are used to pry apart the scales of conifer cones. Then the birds remove the seeds with their tongues. As in so many cases, the adroit eater gets a meal and leaves only the durable package behind, for the next fellow to find empty.

Built-in Sieves

Stabbing, sucking, clawing, gnawing—for many animals, getting dinner is a messy, complicated affair. But for a vast variety of the world's creatures, finding food is as simple as straining spaghetti in a kitchen sieve. Birds, insects, crabs, even marine mammals—all these are among the filter feeders. They strain their food from water, whether a brackish lagoon, a rushing mountain stream, or the generous ocean. Their numbers include the largest animal of all time, the blue whale, a titan with a taste for tiny shrimplike krill. The fact that so huge a beast lives on food the size of tidbits

simply proves the efficiency of the filter-feeding method: A blue whale's single meal of these crustaceans weighs a ton or more.

Whales that eat this way are called baleen whales, for the peculiar feathery plates—baleen—that fringe their mouths and actually do the filtering. Baleen whales embrace two groups: the curve-jawed right whales and the straight-jawed rorquals, humpbacks, and gray whales. The first were so named because they were the "right" ones for old-time whalers to chase since they swam slowly and floated after dying. The more elusive rorquals were named after a Scandi-

Its mouth full of food, a humpback whale breaks the surface of Alaska's Glacier Bay. The whale filters fish and tiny crustaceans from polar waters in the summer, but fasts during the long breeding season in southern waters.

FEEDING
THE BODY

Built-in Sieves

navian term for "tube." When whalers laid the great whales out on deck, their pleated throat skin resembled a row of tubes.

In the place of teeth, baleen hangs from the upper jaw in long, thin, parallel plates that are deeply fringed on the edge facing the mouth. Depending on the species, whales have from 500 to 800 of these plates spaced less than half an inch apart. The plates may be up to 14 feet long, and the fringes mesh to form a tangled mat inside the mouth.

To feed, a humpback whale opens its mouth to scoop vast quantities of water—and whatever fish or drifting plankton happen to be in it. The humpback's pleated throat expands, accordion-style, to its maximum capacity. Once the whale has a mouthful of food-laden water, it closes its jaws, compresses its expanded throat, and forces the water out. Now the baleen comes into play: It acts as a sieve, retaining the food while letting the water filter out. The removal of trapped food from the baleen is, of course, impossible to observe, but the huge tongue, weighing as much as two tons, probably plays a role.

Whalebirds—a group of oceanic birds more accurately known as prions—have fringes in their beaks resembling the whale's baleen. These birds also filter plankton quite effectively from sea water. But even they are runners-up to the champion clan of all filter-feeding birds, the flamingos. These stilt-legged fliers inhabit brackish coastal lagoons or inland salt lakes where they sift small animals and plants from water.

The flamingo's massive, downward-curving bill houses a complete set of feeding utensils. Set at an angle along the inside of the top and bottom halves of the beak are rows of wedge-shaped plates. When the beak halves come together, the top and bottom rows of plates interleave, forming a sifting mesh.

To feed, the flamingo drops its head so that the beak hangs upside down. Only the slightest opening remains between the upper and lower halves of the beak, packed

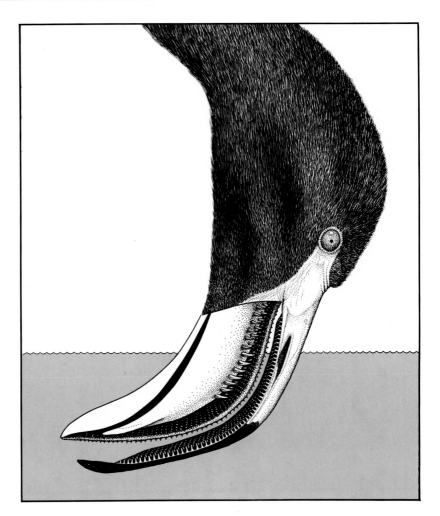

with the food-straining plates. Swinging its head around, the flamingo describes circles in the mud, stirring up its food. At the same time, it opens and closes its beak, sucking in water—and food.

Getting the trapped morsels down the hatch is a job for the flamingo's other tool: a tongue studded with backward-pointing hooks. When it has a mouthful of water and food, the flamingo pushes the water out through the filter with its tongue. As the tongue slides back in, its hooks scrape the food off the plates. Using this tedious in-and-out, suck-and-scrape procedure, a seven-pound flamingo can capture about three-fourths of a pound of food every day.

Whether preening (opposite) or feeding (above), the flamingo's beak works wonders. It is lined with thin, wedge-shaped plates that interlock when the beak is closed to filter food from water.

FEEDING
THE BODY

Built-in Sieves

Among the most diminutive sievers are insects smaller than the larger filter feeders' prey. Some mayflies, caddisflies, and black flies—at one stage or another in their life cycles—sift for food. One variety of young mayfly simply meshes the bristles on its forelegs to snag food carried along by the current of the stream where it lives. Some caddisfly larvae extend their bristle-covered legs from underwater shelters to filter out food particles passing by.

The larval black fly first anchors itself underwater with silken lines and a circle of hooks on its abdomen so that its head faces the current. Then it extends "head fans," wavy streamers rooted between antennae and mouth. The larvae apparently coat these fans with sticky mucus to collect particles that might otherwise slip through.

The black-fly larva's head fans resemble the food-catching antennae of the mole crabs, little crustaceans common along ocean beaches. These animals live where waves break on the shore. As a wave recedes, the mole crab digs itself into the sand, tail first, leaving its feeding antennae exposed. Holding the antennae aloft, the tiny mole crab catches bits of food carried by the spent sea as it flows back.

While mole crabs dig themselves in and out of a new site with each passing wave, tube-building worms build their concrete homes on the seafloor or on mollusk shells. From inside the tube, the worm extends strikingly beautiful gill plumes, feathery organs perhaps three inches across that are adapted for feeding as well as breathing. Tiny, fast-beating threads that cover the plumes force water across the organ. Food particles caught by the plumes flow in a mucous film to the mouth. Also armed with eyespots, the gill plumes retract and disappear if so much as a shadow touches them.

From timid tube worm to fearless whale, fabulous flamingo to flighty mole crab, swimmers, fliers, and sedentary creatures alike have all found fattening ways to sift their food from the waters of the world.

Filter feeders come in all shapes and sizes, but few are more colorful than the "Christmas tree worm" (opposite). The principle of filter feeding—trap your meal with a built-in sieve—is the same whether the creature is a whale or a tiny mole crab (above) or a black-fly larva (top).

FEEDING THE BODY

Communal Banquets

Beauty and beast all in one, the beguiling but deadly Portuguese man-of-war is an assembly of individuals, not a single animal. Some individuals catch prey by shooting out stinging harpoons (1) when touched. Others wrap their mouths around the stunned prey and digest it (2) to feed the community. Honeybees (opposite) are also a colony, every individual working for the benefit of the entire group.

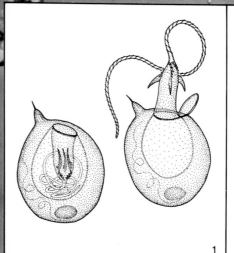

1

2

It is not unusual for a group of animals to band together. The benefits to the herd or the flock are obvious: Labor can be shared and protection is greater. When some creatures band together, however, they do so with unusual conviction.

One such grouping works so smoothly that it is commonly assumed to be a single creature. A relative of the jellyfish, the Portuguese man-of-war is actually an assembly of hundreds of individuals, each one performing a specialized task with a singleness of purpose: keeping the colony alive.

On the other hand, one of the best known animal colonies is easily recognizable as just that—a colony. But if the honeybee colony cannot be mistaken for a single creature, it functions like one. Like the chips in a computer, each member is programmed to carry out a specific task. And just as a chip is meaningless outside the context of the computer, a single bee is purposeless outside the communal context of its hive.

In the man-of-war, two kinds of highly specialized individuals provide and process the food for the colony. Science, in an unusual concession to anthropomorphism, has dubbed them the "stinging persons" and the "feeding persons."

The stinging persons, tentacles trailing below the float, are charged with getting food and defending the colony. For this double duty they are painfully well equipped.

Each tentacle is dotted with masses of tiny stinging cells. Each cell is equipped with its own harpoon—a barbed filament stored coiled and inverted within a lidded pocket. And each cell has its own trigger.

As the man-of-war sails through the ocean, the tentacles, streaming down as far as 30 feet, extend the colony's hunting range down into the ocean. When a fish swims through the tentacle curtain, it trips the triggers of surrounding stinging cells. Lids pop open; harpoons shoot out (see illustration no. 1, page 70). Barbed hooks lash the prey's flesh and lock into the wound. A quick-acting nerve poison paralyzes the prey.

FEEDING THE BODY

Sweet Tooth

Like people in pursuit of luscious calories, many animals have a taste for the sweet. Bees throng around flowers and hummingbirds whirr brightly in front of cuplike blossoms. This we expect. But there are other, less-suspected, nectar seekers. Australian honey possums and several species of bats regularly drop by nature's sweet shops, not just for a treat but for the dulcet food that is the staple of their diet.

The mouse-sized honey possum deftly climbs branches and leaves or hangs upside down by its prehensile tail to reach the flowers that contain its food. Sticking its long, narrow head into each flower, the little marsupial laps up the nectar with a slender, bristle-tipped tongue that extends from its tubelike mouth. Sweet nectar is what lures the tiny possum to the flowers at blossom time, but the dainty nectar-eater sometimes gets a side dish or two: pollen and an occasional insect.

The honey possum has been dubbed the "hummingbird" of the marsupials by some, but the nectar-feeding bats are more deserving of the title. Like the hummingbirds, these airborne mammals fly to their sweet food.

The teeth of some nectar-eating bats are reduced to tiny nubs. After all, teeth are hardly necessary for pursuing a liquid diet. What these bats need most is a lapping tongue, and the tongue of nectar-eating bats is, indeed, a remarkable organ. Tipped with bristles, the tongue can extend to one-fourth the length of the bat. Most nectar-eating bats feed by working their tongues deep into trumpet-shaped flowers and licking the ambrosia within. The Indian short-nosed bat, however, holds onto blossoms with its hind feet and its thumbs, tipping the flower with its weight. As the nectar flows over the petals, the bat drinks the syrup from their surface. Whether hovering like hummingbirds or clenching sturdy stems and petals, the bats move from flower to flower until their stomachs swell like balloons.

But bats do not live by sweets alone. A curious scientist fed captive bats a strict

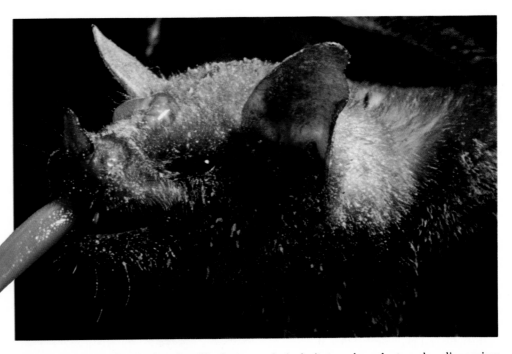

A Sanborn's long-nosed bat (right) displays the tongue that gathers nectar and the fur that harvests pollen. An Australian honey possum (opposite) nose dives into a flower to reach the nectar.

diet of nectar laced with vitamins. The bats died. The survival secret of nectar-eating bats in the wild is a byproduct of their sweet-tooth diets — the bats eat pollen.

In the course of sipping the nectar, the bat inevitably eats some pollen. And, while the bat feeds, its fur gets coated with pollen, which the bat conveniently consumes when it grooms. Unlike the smooth hair of other bats, the hairs of nectar-eaters are rough and prickly, the better to trap the pollen grains. In fact, bats can be dusted so thoroughly with golden pollen that some have been described as a new species: the yellow bat.

The pollen of most plants that attract bats is much richer in protein than the pollen of plants that attract only insects and birds. This "bat pollen" contains an unusual amount of a substance needed to maintain the strong skin in bat wings. And although pollen is difficult to digest, nectar-eating bats have solved that problem. Special glands in their stomachs secrete a powerful acid that breaks down pollen.

Scientists speculate that certain plants and bats co-evolved to their mutual benefit. For example, fruit-eating bats may repay their fruit tree benefactors by dispersing seeds. Nectar-eating bats carry the plant-animal relationship one step further: They directly assure the fertilization of the plants from which they feast. As the bat flits from flower to flower, burying its head in the petals, some of the pollen rubs off on the blossoms and pollinates them.

Scores of plants depend mainly upon bats for pollination. "Bat flowers" grow on the saguaro cactus of the southwestern United States, the wild banana trees in South America, and the baobab tree of Africa. Most of these flowers bloom at night and are white, so the bat can spot them in the dark. Their aroma is pungent, an odor only a bat could love. And their petals and stems are sturdy enough to support a burly bat.

And so, just as nectar and pollen keep the bat alive, so does the pollinating bat keep the plant species proliferating. There is obviously a vital link between bat and flower. Love seems an unlikely word for the plant's relationship to its pollinator. Yet the scientific term for this link — *chiropterophily* — has just that very unscientific meaning: "bat love." How sweet.

FEEDING
THE BODY

Probing Nooks
and Crannies

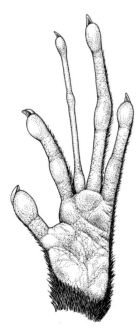

A crane hawk of tropical America hangs from a limb by one foot and pokes inside a hollow with the other. Double-jointed legs let it search the top *and* bottom of the cavity. The aye-aye (left) uses its very thin and nimble middle finger to probe inside holes in logs. The finger pivots on a ball-and-socket joint.

joint. It's that middle finger that spears the grubs, empties eggs, cleans out cracked coconuts, carries water to its mouth—and serves as a toothpick at the end of a meal.

Swift and sharp-eyed, the hawks reign as supreme predators of the skies. But the crane hawks of Latin America and the harrier hawks of Africa do not soar after their prey. Instead, like the woodpecker and the aye-aye, they hunt by poking and probing— often in search of such humble fare as bee larvae and ants. These hawks have double-jointed legs, and they can get to food that other birds of prey cannot reach. A native African name, *Nobwapungu*, describes the hawk's behavior: "beater of hollows." When exploring a hollow in a tree, a hawk hangs with one foot gripping the edge of the hole and the other bending up and down inside the opening to grope for whatever creature is living there.

Some harrier hawks probe bat roosts or cling to bark and poke beneath it for grubs. Others forage in burrows, tree trunks, and rock crevices for frogs, mice, or insects. The West African harrier hawk hangs at the edge of the nest of the weaverbird and rips it open to get at the chicks. Harrier hawks have also been seen hovering like humming-birds while tearing at the weaverbird's nests.

Poking and probing isn't limited to above-ground nooks and crannies, either. Through the tangle of underwater coral jungles swim the small, colorful butterflyfish—some with built-in probes equal to those of any land-locked or airborne creature. Some of these reef-dwellers have been named forceps fish because they use their long, tapering snouts like forceps to reach deep into coral crevices for food.

There may be little of the drama of the hunt when a woodpecker snares an ant, when an aye-aye hooks a grub, when a crane hawk snatches a bat, or when a butterflyfish gobbles a worm. But all are as much a part of the predatory world as the mighty lioness that lunges for a gazelle— all must kill to stay alive.

Nosing about its coral realm, a copperband butterflyfish uses its long snout to probe for small crustaceans and worms living in tiny nooks and crannies. The reef also provides shelter for the colorful fish that is so thin it can escape enemies by slipping into the narrowest cracks.

79

FEEDING THE BODY

Nighttime Prowler

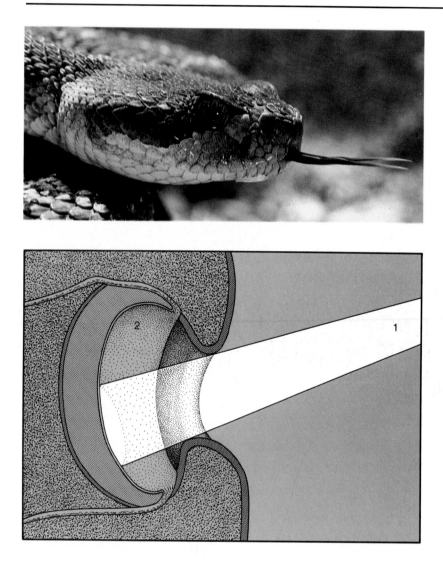

Visible between the eye and nostril of the snake (top), a heat-sensing pit (above) detects the presence of the snake's warm prey. Heat rays (1) from different directions strike different parts of the sensitive membrane (2), sending signals to the brain to map the prey's location.

Imagine a weapon so cleverly designed it can track its victims in the darkest of nights by their body heat alone. Imagine one able to strike so quickly that the human eye cannot see it. Imagine one equipped with so potent a poison that it can paralyze or kill its victims in minutes.

Such weapons exist, not in the missile silos or in the arms storehouses of man, but among the efficient food-getting tools of the pit vipers. This large group of snakes, found in forests, deserts, and grasslands, includes the North American rattlesnakes, water moccasin, and copperhead.

Pit vipers take their name from a pair of indentations in their facial bones, one on each side of the head between the eye and nostril. These harmless-looking pits are actually the gateways to the most marvelous temperature-sensitive organs known.

The pit organs can register heat from a source a foot-and-a-half away—spelling doom for an unsuspecting mouse. The secret of these organs' heat-sensing ability is in their structure. Halfway into the pit cavity stretches a very thin membrane—about one-fourth the thickness of this page—with a rich network of heat-sensitive nerve endings behind it. As the membrane is warmed by a heat source, the nerves send signals to the brain, alerting the snake to a potential meal. But the pits do more than tell the snake that a morsel is near; they also tell it exactly where the meal is.

Because the pit's opening is much smaller than the surface of the membrane, heat rays entering the pit strike only a portion of the membrane's surface, quite a bit the way a beam of light will strike only a portion of the film in a pinhole camera. Accordingly, heat rays coming from different directions will warm different parts of the membrane, stimulating different nerve endings (see illustration). The nerve endings send messages to the brain, creating an accurate temperature map of the snake's surroundings.

All pit vipers are poisonous. They kill their victims by injecting them with a potent venom pumped through long, hollow fangs attached to their hinged upper jaws. The fangs are so long that if they were fixed in place the snake would have either to live with its mouth eternally open or to poison itself the first time it closed its mouth. To avoid this untimely end, a viper's upper jaw is hinged. As the snake closes its mouth, the jaw rotates, tucking the fangs safely out of the way. Muscles pull the jaw and fangs forward as the snake strikes.

After biting a victim, the snake usually backs off and waits patiently for it to die. And patience the viper can well afford, for the dying animal leaves a telltale trail for the snake to follow. The viper's tracking tool, its forked tongue, is no less remarkable than its heat-sensing equipment.

The snake's tongue is not an organ of taste like the human's; it extends the snake's sense of smell. Flicking in and out of the snake's mouth, the forked tongue picks up chemical particles from the air and the ground. The snake then delivers the microscopic clues on the prongs of its tongue to two openings on the roof of its mouth. The openings lead to two cavities which form the Jacobson's organ, a highly sensitive structure with nerve endings similar to those in a human's nose. This half-taste, half-smell organ keeps the snake on the trail of the dying prey.

When it approaches its now-quiet meal, the snake uses its tongue again, flicking it over the prey's body to determine the location of its head. A viper usually swallows its food head first; the package goes down more easily that way. But the viper's work is not over, for its prey is likely to be bigger around than the snake's head.

The snake has no cutting or grinding teeth with which to slice its food into smaller pieces. To swallow an oversized meal, the snake has no alternative but to open its mouth wide—very wide. As the mouth opens, a hinge connecting the lower jaw to the skull pivots, letting the rear of the lower jaw drop down. In addition, a ligament at the front of the lower jaw lets it spread sideways, further widening the gape. The snake then creeps its jaws forward around the meal; first one side of the lower jaw moves forward, then the other, until the victim is engulfed. To prevent the snake from suffocating while its mouth is full, the opening to the windpipe, the glottis, moves forward and out of the snake's mouth until the swallowing is done.

The snake is custom-built for its role in nature, so it seems odd that human beings have for so long pictured it as a creature of evil. Its goal in life is one we all share, one nature has well equipped it for: to survive.

Frozen in its lethal lunge, a western diamondback rattler aims its deadly fangs at an unseen victim. A drop of venom glistens on the fangs' needle-sharp points. Normally folded back, the fangs spring forward to deliver their deadly contents. The fangs sometimes break, but no matter—new ones soon take their place.

FEEDING
THE BODY

Living Lures

Aesop, in his fable about the wolf in sheep's clothing, warned that appearances can be deceiving. But another Greek, Plato, said there was more to deception than pulling the wool over someone's eyes. "Everything that deceives," he wrote, "may be said to enchant." Beguiling predators throughout the animal kingdom use that technique—attraction through delusion—to get prey. Snakes, turtles, fish, and spiders are among the deceivers that lure victims with bait too good to be true.

Since the Garden of Eden, snakes have had a reputation for deception. Some, such as the American copperhead, practice the art. A young copperhead hides itself under a carpet of leaves, sticks out the yellow tip of its tail, and wriggles it like a worm. A frog or other hungry victim heads for a likely meal but becomes one instead. Another deceiver, the sand boa of northern Africa and the Middle East, uses the same stunt in another arena. This brownish snake burrows into the sand, leaving only its wriggling tail exposed to lure passing rodents. Although passersby can be few and far between in the desert, the snake awaits them breathlessly, literally without breathing, its nostrils sealed tight against the loose sand.

The alligator snapping turtle fishes the rivers of the southeastern United States with patience and skill that human anglers would envy. Attached to its tongue is a fleshy pink lure that to a fish looks like a live worm. The turtle goes fishing by sitting motionlessly on the bottom, camouflaged by its dark color and the algae that grow on its shell. Opening its mouth wide, it wriggles its lure to entice curious victims to swim in. The snapper, which may weigh more than 200 pounds, does not snap up alligators, as its name implies; but it does catch small turtles as well as fish. The snapper augments its bide-and-bite diet with vegetation and scrap scavenged from the bottom.

The decoyfish, like other scorpionfish, has fin spines that carry venom. But this rare fish has something else, too, indicated

by both its common and its scientific name, *Iracundus signifer,* "irritable sign-bearer." On closer inspection, the sign is a decoy, a dorsal fin that looks like a tiny fish, complete with a mouth and an eye.

When the decoyfish spots a potential meal, it raises its dorsal fin and lies still, stopping even the movement of its gill flaps. As the dorsal fin rises, it changes from a drab part of the mottled body to what looks like a small red fish. A dark spot on the fin enlarges to resemble an eye, and an indenta-

Built-in lures bring the meals home: A camouflaged alligator snapping turtle (opposite) hunts with the tantalizing pink lure on its tongue. A fishy fin (top) tricks the decoyfish's prey into swimming near its mouth.

FEEDING THE BODY

Living Lures

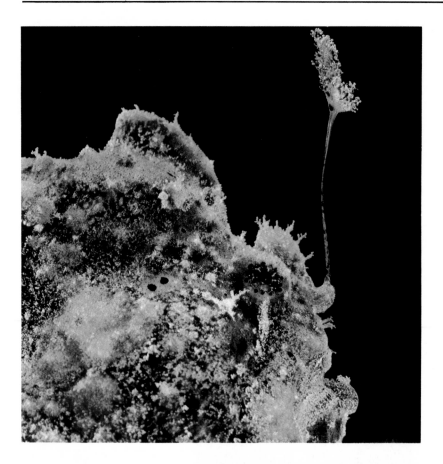

tion in the fin takes the shape of a mouth. The real fish then wriggles its fin, making the illusion even more complete. When the victim approaches its expected meal, the deceiver grabs and eats the meal-seeker. Then the decoyfish refolds the fooling fin, which returns to its former color.

Much more common than the decoyfish is the anglerfish. There are about 225 species of anglerfish. The largest—weighing more than 40 pounds—are members of a bottom-dwelling family.

If little fish dream, the anglerfish is their nightmare. Just swimming by a camouflaged anglerfish can mean death. When the anglerfish opens its mouth quickly, it creates a vacuum that sucks in water, transforming a fish-filled sea into a bouillabaisse flowing into the anglerfish. Its mouth is jammed with long, sharp, backward-curving teeth that form a cage. The teeth are hinged and fold back to admit extra-large prey. But, like a turnstile, the teeth do not turn the other way. The only exit is into the angler's maw.

Most fish don't get close to the anglerfish by accident. The anglerfish lures them with

An anglerfish fishes with a transparent pole fitted with a fleshy flap for bait. Originally part of the angler's dorsal fin, the rod can be lowered and raised, alluringly twitching the bait.

a fishing pole sprouting from the top of its head. A bit of tissue that looks like a worm dangles from the top of the fishing pole. The fish lowers the top of the pole until the artificial lure lines up with its mouth. The anglerfish then moves the pole and wriggles the lure until a curious fish happens by.

The anglerfish begins life with a normal fin on its back. As the fish grows, a few of the front rays detach from the rest of the fin and migrate to the top of the head. The front ray becomes the fishing pole and a bit of tissue that had been part of the webbing of the fin now becomes the lure. The converted ray is attached to muscles that the fish uses to wield its fishing pole.

The anglerfish takes its time while fishing and does not waste any motion. The fish finds a likely spot and settles into a shallow depression that it scoops out with its pelvic fins. The fish's drab, knobby body blends with the seafloor that is its home. A fringe around its body blurs the line between fish and terrain. Bottom-dwelling anglerfish have extremely small gill openings and breathe slowly. They expend little energy, and their sedentary form of fishing fits their life style.

The nocturnal bolas spider, contrary to the adage, does not a tangled web weave in order to deceive. The bolas spider merely spins one short line. Suspended from the line is a sticky ball. The spider holds the line with one front leg and, like a South American gaucho hurling a bolas, swings the ball at a target, usually a moth. After catching the insect, the spider paralyzes it with a bite and stores it away in a silk shroud.

The bolas spider lures victims by secreting what to a male moth seems to be the scent of a female moth. Male moths, darting toward a mate that is not there, dart instead into the deadly radius of the spider's bolas.

The bolas spider successfully lures two or three moths a night. This is about the number of victims a web-spinning spider snares each day as, unlike the tricksters that live by being not what they seem to be, it weaves but does not deceive.

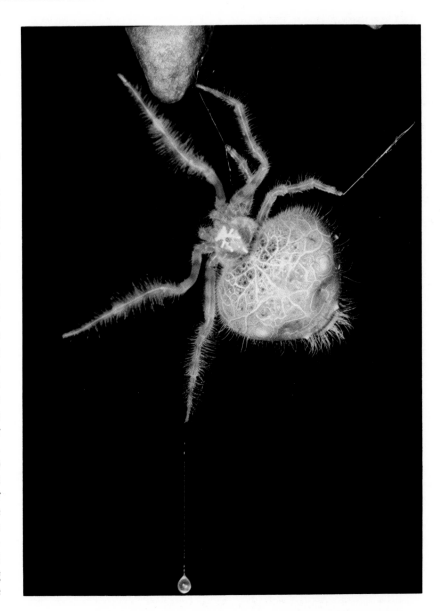

The bolas spider snares its food with a combination of string, glue, and perfume. Copying the scent of a female moth, the spider lures lovesick males into killing range. The spider then slings a sticky pearl on a lustrous line to catch its prey.

FEEDING
THE BODY

Whooooo! **Whooooooo!** For ages, this noise has chilled listeners to the bone. In folklore, the owl's sonorous cry has always been the voice of doom. Merely the bird's presence on a rooftop makes the people inside quake from fear that a death is near.

Today, such stories are easily dismissed as quaint myth. But while as a rule the events in folklore are fictional, the tales often bear a nugget of truth. When an owl perches on a rooftop, people need not panic. But when an owl perches in a treetop, the mouse scurrying beneath has good reason to fear for its life.

In its natural habitat, the owl lives up to its death-knell reputation—no folk fantasy about it. For the owl is an expert hunter, adept at prying into the night's recesses and discovering the life within. The night holds few secrets from the owl.

Nocturnal owls can see in near-total darkness. Unlike the round orbs of human eyes, owl eyes are tubular and extend deep into the head: The bigger the eyes, the more light they can gather. The eyes of the largest owls are bigger than human eyes and are so sensitive they need only one-hundredth of the light humans need to see. There is a price to be paid for such powers, however. The owl's eyes are so huge that there is no space in the skull for muscles to move them. Without turning its head, the owl can see only straight in front of itself.

But sacrifices made for one amazing ability are often offset by another ability. In the owl's case, the neck is highly flexible and makes up for the immobile eyes. Four-teen vertebrae—twice the number in a human's neck—enable the owl to turn its head nearly upside down and to swivel it three-quarters of the way around.

Because of this remarkable flexibility, misconception has credited the owl with an even more amazing ability. Many people believe it can rotate its head around and around and that it is in danger of unscrewing its head if it circles too much.

Of course this isn't true, but the owl can easily fool observers by snapping its head around so quickly that it appears to have completed a circle.

When the owl turns its head to scan for food, it searches not only with its large eyes, but also with its ears. Although less obvious than the owl's famous eyes, its ears are equally impressive.

Most animals – man included – hear sounds in the range of their own vocalizations. So does the owl – but it also hears the high-pitched sounds of its rodent prey. A barn owl can catch a mouse in total darkness by focusing on the mouse's minute squeakings, sounds much higher pitched than any of the owl's utterings.

The ears' sensitivity comes from their unusual design. The ears of most birds, including owls, are small openings on either side of the head. But unlike the ears of other birds, those of nocturnal owls are asymmetrical. The right and left openings have different shapes, and one ear is higher on the head than the other. This enables the owl to pinpoint the source of a sound.

Many animals, including owls and humans, locate the source of a sound by comparing differences in the loudness and time of arrival of the sound in each ear. The ears must be a certain distance apart before the system works very well, and the

owl's broad head meets the requiremen[t] admirably. Since both human ears are a[t] the same height on the head, people ca[n] tell if a sound is coming from the right o[r] the left, but not from high or low. That'[s] where the owl's lopsided ears give it a[n] advantage. They can locate the dinner be[ll] no matter where it rings.

The disc of feathers framing an owl'[s] face adds to this hunter's hearing abilit[y.] The feathers cover long vertical flaps [of] flesh that run from the top of the skull t[o] the bottom jaw. Owls erect the flaps to cu[t] the ear from the front, funneling sounds i[n] from behind.

Because the victims of the nocturna[l] owls are also nocturnal, many of the[m] have excellent hearing for avoiding thei[r] pursuers. To counter this, the owl has ye[t] another talent that gives it an edge over it[s] prey: Its feathers are modified so the ow[l] flies almost soundlessly. Unlike the feath[-] ers of most birds, which have hard edge[s,] the owl's feathers have delicately fringe[d] edges. This fringe deadens the noise of ai[r] rushing over the wing.

The owl's silent flight is facilitated by it[s] light weight. Even large owls weigh rela[-] tively little; most of their bulk is feathers. A[] barn owl, for instance, tips the scales a[t] barely one pound. Because an owl's weigh[t] is slight in relation to its wing size, it i[s] easily buoyed up by the wind, reducing th[e] amount of noisy wing flapping needed t[o] stay aloft. This cloak of silence keeps tel[l-] tale rodent squeaks audible, guiding th[e] owl to its meal. With no warning of th[e] owl's approach, the prey has little chanc[e] to escape before it is too late.

As the owl strikes, its sharp, outstretche[d] talons lead the attack. The force of th[e] impact and the weight of the owl flex th[e] legs. Tendons leading to the feet tighten a[s] they are pulled by the bending legs, auto[-] matically snapping the talons shut. If th[e] prey struggles, the talons are driven deepe[r] into its flesh. Clearly it is nature that ha[s] invented the better mousetrap.

A horizontal section of an owl's head (below) reveals its nighttime hunting equipment: huge, tubular eyes to gather images in the dark; deeply cut, asymmetrical ear cavities to scoop sounds and pinpoint their source. A great horned owl's mousetrap talons automatically clamp to hold its prey (opposite).

STAYING ALIVE

Disappearing Act

While the zebra's bold stripes would seem to draw attention to the animal in the evenly colored African plains where it lives, their very vividness is what gives them the power to deceive. When zebras stand in a large herd, as they often do, the repeating stripes make it difficult for a stalking predator to tell where one zebra ends and another begins. When a herd fans out in panic during an attempted ambush, the zebras create an even greater chaos of stripes by bolting in all directions. The predator may slow in confusion for only a portion of a second, but that slight pause may be long enough to save a zebra from becoming dinner.

Even if a predator has managed to single out an individual animal to attack, the stripes may still aid the zebra. Wider stripes on its haunches create the optical illusion that the rear half of the zebra is closer to the predator than the front is. This illusion may make the predator misjudge the distance to its quarry, allowing the zebra to escape, if only by a fraction of an inch.

The zebra's stripes also act as more traditional camouflage. At dawn and dusk, when the chance of lion and hyena attack is greatest, the stripes blend into an almost uniform gray, and the zebra is concealed in the twilight. And when the zebra stands in sunlit, tall grasses, the pattern of sun and shadow and white and black make this conspicuous animal disappear.

In other animals, the ability to disappear is almost a literal one. The glasswing butterfly, the glass catfish, the transparent shrimp, and many other small insects and sea creatures have wings or bodies so transparent that they allow light to shine through. Even if certain internal organs or structures are visible to a predator, these phantoms are apt to be overlooked since their overall body shape cannot be distinguished.

Conventionally camouflaged animals have colors and markings that enable them to blend into their background by approximating its appearance. This form of camouflage is complicated immensely, however,

Nature's camouflage techniques span a vast spectrum. A zebra herd's bold stripes create an optical illusion that hides individuals (previous page). The absence of color protects a glasswing butterfly and a transparent shrimp: The background is visible while the animals disappear.

Camouflage is the art of refined inconspicuousness, an art that has almost as many forms as nature has colors. It works on a simple principle: An animal not seen is an animal not eaten. Typically, an animal becomes invisible to the eyes of a predator by blending in with the colors of its background, but there are other ways of hiding in plain sight. Some animals have transparent bodies that let the background show through, making their bodies disappear. Yet an animal need not be unobtrusive to gain protection. Even the eyecatching stripes of the zebra are a form of camouflage.

STAYING ALIVE

Portable Shelters

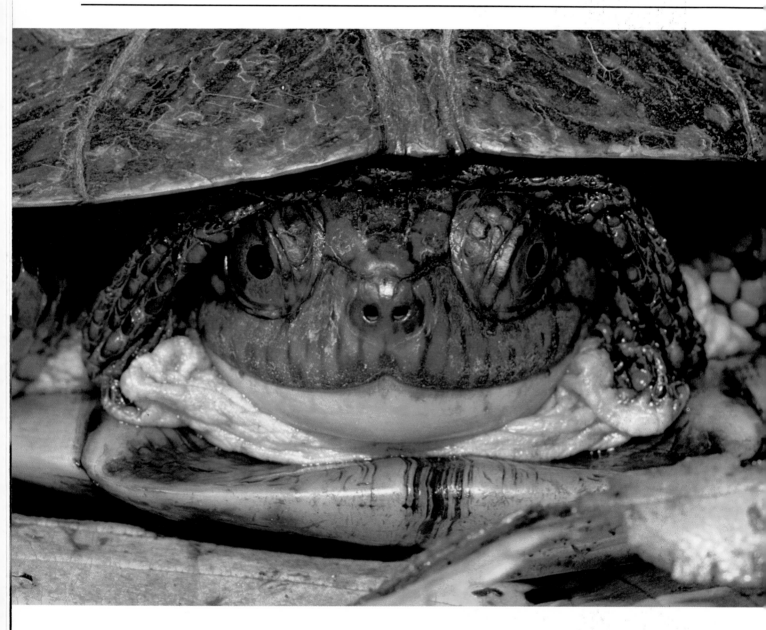

Hiding from its enemies, a Blanding's turtle makes its portable shelter into a fortress. The hinged underside allows the front and the back of the shell to be closed tightly.

Home, for some animals, is where the heart is — and the stomach, and the brain, and everything else. The home-body animals make refuges of their bodies or tote borrowed abodes. Either way, they go through life carrying portable shelters. Their home-bodies are their castles.

Turtles tuck their heads and feet into their armor in times of trouble. Armadillos, pangolins, and tiny millipedes roll their bodies into armor-plated fortresses. Hermit crabs adopt shell homes made by snails.

The most apparent part of a turtle's armor is the upper part of its shell, the carapace. It is part of the animal's skeleton, not merely an accessory that encloses the body. The bony carapace is the backbone and rib cage. The bones that support the legs are connected to the inside of the rib-cage roof. In most turtles, the lower part of the shell, the

plastron, is attached to the carapace at the sides but not at the back and front. As the turtle grows, so does its shell. And, unlike the homes of humans, a slightly damaged turtle shell can repair itself.

A turtle's rigid shell produces a problem analogous to that of a person tightly bound by a stiff corset—how to breathe? The turtle's ingenious architecture solves that problem niftily by including an unusual air pump for breathing. Muscles on each side of the turtle's body contract to enlarge the body cavity around the lungs, thereby creating a vacuum and sucking air into the body. The turtle exhales by contracting another set of muscles to squeeze its internal organs against the lungs and force the air out. It is as if the turtle continuously gives itself artificial respiration.

Some turtles breathe underwater by absorbing oxygen through the skin that lines the mouth or by pumping water through the anus and into special sacs that extract oxygen from the water.

The box turtle is one of a group of turtles that can withdraw completely into their shells and tightly close them to hide. Its bottom shell is hinged so that it can be tightly folded against the upper one to seal the body inside. A box turtle can pull its head and long neck into its shell because its neck vertebrae have highly flexible joints. These joints enable the turtle to fold its neck into an "S" suspended from the top of the shell (see illustration). In other turtles, legs, tails, and sometimes portions of their necks remain

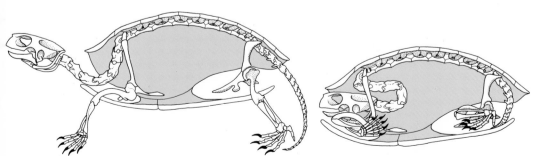

The box turtle closes up when an inquisitive opossum noses around. The illustrations show how a turtle's extended head and legs (far left) can be drawn inside the shell (left). Unusually flexible joints are the turtle's secret.

STAYING ALIVE

Portable Shelters

Rolling, rolling, rolled—a three-banded armadillo performs its disappearing act. It usually walks on the tips of its claws (above). Elastic skin between the plates on its back enable it to protect its soft underparts by forming a ball (opposite, top). When balled up (opposite, bottom), triangular shields protect its head and tail.

exposed because their shells cannot snap shut. These turtles protect their heads by bending them to the side and drawing them next to the shell.

If a turtle may be said to resemble a tank, the armadillo may be thought of as a knight in rolling armor. When threatened, an armadillo quickly coils into a ball, covering its soft underparts with its hard shell. Its armor consists of numerous rigid, horny plates with enough pliable skin between them to permit the armadillo to bend its body.

Armadillos range in size from 120-pound giants of the Amazon to the six-inch-long fairy armadillos of Argentina and Bolivia. Loosely attached along its back, the fairy armadillo's armor resembles a pink cape draped over a wispy, long-haired body. The fairy's rump is also armored. Instead of rolling into a ball when threatened, this quick

creature dives into its burrow or digs one furiously. Then it neatly plugs its underground refuge with its armored rear end.

Of the 20 armadillo species, the three-banded armadillo of South America is the only one that can roll up into a tight ball. Others, such as the common long-nosed armadillo of Florida and the southwestern United States, are not quite flexible enough to form a perfect sphere.

Like the armadillo, the armor-covered pangolin (from the Malay word for *roller*) uses a roll-up defense against predators—with an added motherly touch. When danger lurks, a pangolin mother carrying a baby on her back shifts the baby to her front and rolls it up inside the ball.

Mollusks like limpets, snails, and whelks carry permanent homes built of home-grown chemicals. The substances ooze, layer upon

layer, from the edge of the mantle, the fold of tissue that encloses the animal's inner organs. Symmetrical mollusks, such as limpets, produce shell material around the entire edge of the mantle at a steady rate, and the result is a pyramidal shell. Other species, such as whelks, ooze material at different rates from each side of the mantle: The result is a spiral shell. Each of the 60,000 species of mollusks has its own variation on the home-building theme.

The mollusk known as the chambered nautilus builds a dwelling so magnificent that it has inspired several famous poets. But the mollusk, ever moving from old chamber to new, is a migrant in a mansion. The poets could have written as well of the humble hermit crab, which, on the move like the tenant of the wondrously complex nautilus shell, earns a place to live in through constant, silent toil.

The hermit crab is a body in continual search of a home. A hermit begins life as a free-swimming larva. When it becomes a juvenile, it is large enough to be noticeable — and imperiled. A soft, vulnerable creature with no built-in protection, the young hermit then starts its first search for a vacant shell to inhabit.

As the crab grows, it must find larger and larger lodgings, and so house-hunting becomes a way of life. Over the eons, various species of hermit crabs have developed an affinity for particular shells: long hermit crabs with coiled abdomens, for example, choose long, tightly spiraled homes.

Most hermit crabs have lost some of the short legs on the abdomen, making it easier for them to fit inside shells. Furthermore, in some species, the abdomen itself is permanently twisted to one side so that the animal can slip into a spiraled shell. The twist is to the right for species that inhabit homes spiraling rightwards and to the left for species living in homes that spiral in the other direction.

When a hermit wants to move about, it drags its home along by pressing non-skid

STAYING ALIVE

Sensing Danger

A kangaroo rat stops to listen for a predator's approach. Its hearing is especially tuned to pick up the faint, low-pitched sounds of a swooping owl or a rustling rattlesnake—the kangaroo rat's greatest enemies.

It has been said that eternal vigilance is the price of liberty. But for some creatures, it is the price of life itself. Animals that run the risk of becoming food for others must exercise the utmost caution when they venture out of hidden places to find food for themselves. Their survival depends upon keen senses that can detect the sudden, nearly imperceptible movements of predators.

For the kangaroo rat of the arid southwestern United States and northern Mexico, sharp hearing acts as an early warning system. The nocturnal kangaroo rat is a small, seed-eating rodent so named because of powerful hind legs on which it hops, kangaroo fashion, across the desert. Its modest-sized external ears belie the amazing hearing apparatus hidden inside the skull.

As in other mammals, the kangaroo rat's middle ears are encased in rounded, bony structures called the auditory bullae. In the kangaroo rat, however, these structures are so large that their combined size is greater than that of its brain.

The large volume of airspace enclosed

by these structures contributes to the kangaroo rat's excellent hearing. Sound waves hitting the eardrums, which cover the openings to the bony structures, cause them to compress the air behind them. The more airspace there is, the more easily compression can take place—just as it is easier to squeeze a large balloon than a small one into a different shape.

Low-pitched sounds produce the greatest compression, and it's not mere coincidence that the kangaroo rat's ears are well designed to hear sounds of this type: Some very low-pitched sounds spell the greatest danger for the kangaroo rat. The muffled wingbeats of an owl swooping down for the kill, the rasping of a rattlesnake's scales against the ground just before it strikes—sounds too low pitched for easy detection by human ears come across loud and clear to a kangaroo rat. And, with a sudden, precisely timed leap, it often evades even these stealthy predators.

Eyesight is as important to some creatures as hearing is to the kangaroo rat. Animals that must keep an eye out for predators typically have eyes located on the sides of narrow heads, so that they can survey much of their surroundings without turning their heads.

The woodcock, a bird of swampy woodlands and thickets, makes the broadest possible use of this adaptation: It can see a full 360 degrees around itself. The woodcock's eyes are not only far to the sides but also toward the top if its head, allowing the bird to look straight above as well. Thus it can be feeding—its long beak probing the mud—and still scan for signals telling of the approach of a predator from any direction, including from the sky.

Hunters—such as owls and cats and people—are better served by eyes placed forward on the head. Their placement creates a large overlap in the area that each eye sees. Binocular vision, as this is called,

enables the animal to judge distance—the better to swoop or pounce with accuracy.

Sometimes the hunter is in turn the hunted. One such animal is the tarsier, a small nocturnal creature of the Southeast Asian forests. This cousin of the monkeys has enormous eyes—so big that they are the largest eyes in proportion to body size of any animal. With these remarkable peepers, the tarsier searches for a succulent insect or lizard which it snares with a lightning-fast leap and a grab.

No animal can see in total darkness, but the tarsier's huge eyes use whatever meager light is available. The light-receptor cells in its retina (the interior back surface of the eyeball) are rod cells—the type most sensitive to dim light. Cone cells, found in the eyes of many animals living in bright light, are absent from the tarsier's eye.

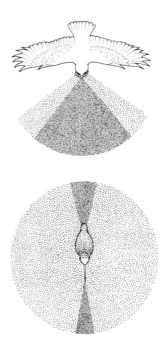

A woodcock hiding in foliage (left) uses more than camouflage to stay alive. It has a 360-degree field of vision (bottom illustration, light area), and can judge distances in front or back (dark area). The woodcock can see predators all around itself. In contrast, an owl (top illustration) can judge distances over a broader area (dark area) but has a narrower field of vision (light area). The owl's eyesight is designed for seeing prey; the woodcock's, for seeing its enemies.

STAYING ALIVE

Sensing Danger

To supplement its eyesight, the tarsier also has highly sensitive hearing. It can crinkle and twist its ears in different directions to pinpoint a sound's source. However, because its eyes are smack on the front of its face, the tarsier must turn its head to follow movement. Because it has an extremely flexible neck, it can swivel its head around to look directly behind its back.

The same adaptations which make the tarsier an efficient hunter can help protect it when the tables are turned. With predatory treetop neighbors like owls, palm civets, and arboreal snakes around, it's handy to be able—by merely a twist of the neck—to see what's approaching from behind.

If the tarsier's motto is "the bigger the better" when it comes to eyes, the scallop's is certainly "the more the merrier." A scallop has about 60 tiny eyes evenly spaced along its mantle. When the mollusk opens its two shells even slightly, its eyes peer out like a row of glittering jewels.

The most remarkable thing about the scallop's eyes isn't their number; rather, it's that each eye contains a tiny mirror made of layer upon layer of very thin film. It is the mirror, located back of the retina, rather than the lens, located in front of it, which focuses images onto the retina's light-sensitive cells.

The image produced on the retina by the mirror is gray and indistinct. Because there is no sharp contrast between dark and light areas in the image, the scallop has a rather foggy view of its world. Nevertheless, the mirror eye can detect motion. And if a scallop perceives danger moving its way, it can—depending on the species—bury itself in the sand or swim away by clapping its shells together, like runaway castanets.

It is still a mystery to scientists why the scallop has so many eyes. The entire visual field could be covered by many fewer. Perhaps, if you're as tasty a morsel as a scallop and live among a clutter of sand, pebbles, and weeds, it's a good idea to be on the lookout for trouble—in a big way.

Looking out for danger gives early warning to animals on land and in the sea. The big-eyed tarsier (above) supplements its excellent night vision with a head that turns nearly a full circle. Each of the scallop's 60 blue eyes (right) can detect the slightest threatening shadow.

Alert!

A Thomson's gazelle grazing on the grasslands of Kenya pauses from its meal and looks about, its eyes and ears ever alert to the threat of hungry predators. This time danger is present—a lioness, ambling through the nearby brush. But surprisingly, instead of running away, the gazelle walks toward the lioness, though still keeping a safe distance. After a few tense moments the gazelle stops. Now it turns and bounds away, taking peculiar, stiff-legged leaps, flashing a snowy white rump.

The gazelle's unusual leaping—called "stotting"—is meant to be obvious, alerting others in the herd to the nearby danger. It possibly serves other purposes as well. Some behavioral scientists believe that the gazelle may be testing the lioness to determine whether she is ready to attack. If the lioness does not respond to the confrontation and the stotting by giving chase, the gazelle simply resumes grazing. After all, there is no need to waste time and energy running if there is nothing chasing it.

Obviously, getting food is a dangerous and time-consuming occupation for all grazers. Tall grasses may mean dinner, but they also mean cover for prowling predators. So the grazers have two big chores: Eat as much as possible, and keep an eye out for danger. It would help if animals that spot danger could spread the word. And that is just what they do by stotting, flashing their rump hairs, and heeding the alarm calls of birds or other animals.

By flashing bright tail hairs, stotting grazers give a visual warning to the members of the herd. At the same time, the animals may be distracting their pursuers. A rabbit, apparently with no other rabbit to warn, runs with its white tail exposed and flashing as the animal darts from side to side. Observers have suggested that the rabbit actually goads the pursuer into giving chase. Then, as the pursuer focuses intently on the flashing white signal, the rabbit suddenly stops and sits on its white tail, showing only its brown back. With the white target no longer visible, the pursuer loses track of its prey and turns away.

Animals of several different species may eat together and share, if not the food, at least the responsibility of watching for predators. Giraffes contentedly graze on thorny acacia trees and swift impalas graze on savannah grasses, relying on the tick birds feeding on their backs to give early warning of any danger the birds might spot.

Many birds in flocks warn each other of danger with a signal that other species can also recognize: a single, high-pitched whistle or squeaky sound that is very difficult for predators to locate. But making sounds is not the only way to warn others of impending danger. Some fish spread the alarm by releasing a special "fear" scent into the water when they are attacked and bitten. At the first whiff of this scent, the surviving fish react in whatever way works best: schooling, fleeing separately, or suddenly ceasing all motion. But whatever the response or sort of creature, the alert signals of an individual animal often save the day, not merely for itself, but also for other animals nearby.

Hightailing away from an enemy, a rabbit flashes its white tail. The predator chasing the rabbit may fix its gaze on the white spot. When the rabbit suddenly stops and sits on its tail, the predator loses sight of the spot—and its prey.

Alert!

Impalas bound away from danger with prodigious leaps. White patches on their rumps signal *alert!* to herd members.

Advertising Trouble

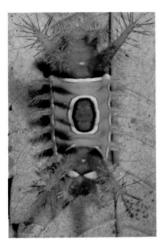

The bright colors of the poison dart frog (left) warn predators of its potent poison. Through experience, predators learn to leave the frog in peace. The prominent patch on the poisonous saddleback caterpillar (above) provides the same kind of protection.

If you've got it, flaunt it, the saying goes. That is a philosophy the family of poison dart frogs knows well. Most other frogs are protectively shaded in earthen tones of green and brown and are most active under the protection of night. The poison dart frogs go about their business only in broad daylight when their flamboyant stripes and spots of yellow, orange, blue, and other bright colors show up best.

The apparent confidence of these frogs comes from something intended to be obvious—painfully so—to their enemies. The frogs are poisonous. To make sure their enemies are aware of this, they advertise their poison by flaunting their brilliantly colored skin that tells predators, *beware!* Thus securely cloaked, these frogs nonchalantly amble through places where their nontoxic kin would literally fear to tread.

The poison dart frogs' poisons are secreted by glands in their skin and vary in toxicity from species to species. Some poisons merely taste bad, others burn or numb the lining of the mouth, and some are so potent that even touching the frog's skin can be dangerous for a predator.

Yet even the strongest of these poisons cannot keep all enemies away. Some snakes and large spiders are apparently immune to it. And the poison actually attracts one predator—man.

The poison dart frogs take their name from a role they unwittingly play in poisoning the blow darts some South American Indians use in hunting. The Indians gather the frogs and torment them to make them release large quantities of frothy poison. Then the Indians rub their arrowheads across the backs of the frogs to coat them with a deadly film that sometimes remains potent for a full year's hunting. Some Indians still hunt this way.

Although limited to South America and southern Central America, these poisonous frogs flourish in their forest habitat, testimony to the success of their survival strategy, one that a number of other animals share.

The poisonous fire-bellied toad of Europe, for one, spends much of its time in the water. The toad is drab gray on top, but its underside is vividly splashed with orange, a warning to fish and turtles beneath it to stay away. If surprised by a predator while on land, like a gymnast, the toad quickly does a backbend to expose the warning marks on its belly until the predator retreats.

Another seemingly innocuous animal, the saddleback caterpillar, has what appears to be the bull's-eye of a target on its back. But the marking, in fact, helps keep the creature from becoming the target of a hungry predator. This marking, too, is an advertisement of poison. The caterpillar is covered with sharp, hollow spines connected to poison glands in its body. When a predator grips the caterpillar, the tips of the spines break off and the poison is released. The poison, which stings worse than that of stinging nettle, teaches the predator not to try *that* meal again.

A variety of mammals also use attention-getting advertisements for defense, but unlike the brightly colored frogs and caterpillars, the mammals are mostly nocturnal and are not poisonous. Since color is ill-perceived at night, bright, colorful warning markings would be ineffective. These creatures, then, carry the markings that show up most boldly in darkness: bright white stripes and spots on black backgrounds.

The best known of these is the skunk, whose white stripes and blotches advertise its powerful stench. The smelly spray is not only offensive to man and animal alike, but is irritating to the eyes if squirted into them. Other nocturnal animals such as the polecat and the badger have similar methods of defense, though their spray is much less potent. And the porcupine advertises its prickly form of protection with striking black-and-white bands on its quills.

While warning markings vary greatly among animals that are poisonous or irritating to predators, their message is clear: Leave me alone, or you'll be sorry.

STAYING ALIVE

Starting Over

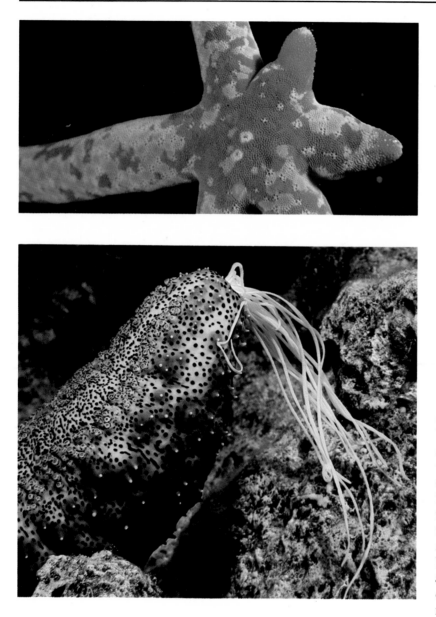

A budding beauty, this starfish sprouts new arms to replace two lost ones. Below, a sea cucumber, called "cotton spinner," ejects its stringy white innards to entangle an enemy. The innards will grow back.

On storm-wracked clipper ships of yesteryear, seasoned captains threw valuable cargo overboard to save their vessels. In airline disaster movies, the pilot orders the flight crew to jettison baggage and cargo when an engine fails. In nature's less romanticized emergencies, astonishing numbers of creatures abandon parts of themselves in last-ditch efforts to preserve their precious lives—and then grow the parts back!

Regeneration of body parts is most common among the invertebrates. Starfish, the spiny daisies of the sea, actually benefit from this ability. Fragmentation helps them reproduce, as each separated arm—so long as it comes away with a part of the central disc—will grow into a complete starfish. Because starfish thrive on oysters and clams, oystermen used to slice the stars in two whenever they caught them, meaning to kill them off. But by dividing the starfish, oystermen multiplied their own problems.

Like its relative the starfish, the long, slippery sea cucumber also routinely takes leave of important body parts. But sea cucumbers carry this defensive measure to extremes, actually discharging internal organs. When under attack, a sea cucumber ejects masses of sticky, white tubules through its anus. Swelling and elongating in the water, the tubules can entangle a crab or other predator so well that it dies trapped like a fly in a spider web, while the sluggish sea cucumber creeps away to reproduce more tubules at leisure. If need be, the cucumber ejects its digestive organs, respiratory organs, and gonads. All can be spared until they regenerate.

The lobster, another invertebrate, sometimes responds to attack by parting company with a large claw. A disembodied pincer clasps the enemy even more tightly than if it were still attached, while the lobster scrambles from the continuing fray. Slowly, with each molt, the claw regenerates.

The ability to regenerate parts is much less common among the vertebrates than among the lower animals. Only salamanders, tadpoles, and lizards can do it. How, then,

Two "glass snakes" grow new tail tips. These legless lizards get their name from their ability to "shatter" their tails in several segments when escaping from a predator. Muscles pinch off a segment at any of several possible locations.

can the shattering of glass snakes—which gives them their name—be explained? Strange though it may seem, glass snakes are really lizards. Legless, it's true, but with all the other characteristics that distinguish lizards from snakes: moveable eyelids, external ear openings, and an unexpandable lower jawbone, to name just three.

The tail of the glass snake, the part behind the anus, constitutes two-thirds of the body length and can snap off in a number of places. Like those of most other lizards, the tails of glass snakes have preformed breaking points. Certain vertebrae easily split in half, the surrounding tissues separate neatly, blood vessels close off, and swelling muscles inhibit bleeding.

The newly severed tails of many lizards continue to thrash about, powered by energy stored in them. Skink tails, for example, can writhe and slap 300 times a minute for five minutes. Usually that movement distracts the predator while the erstwhile owner manages its escape.

The lucky lizard's hind end heals quickly, and a new tail soon replaces the lost one—but it is not an exact duplicate. Instead of individual vertebrae, a cartilaginous tube now protects the spinal cord. The skin is lighter in color and the new tail is often smaller than the original. But the replacement works well enough: for balance, for locomotion, and as a disposable target for passing predators, proving the old adage, "Easy come, easy go."

While no mammal grows back lost limbs, a few species of rodents leave their tails in the jaws of their pursuers—but only once. When in trouble, the spiny rats of Central and South America sacrifice their tails from the fifth vertebra on. Other rodents—including some rats, mice, and squirrels—wriggle out of their tail sheaths, escaping with the underlying bones and muscles that later wither and drop off. While a lost tail can be a serious handicap, especially for species that need their tails for balance, it's better to give up length than life!

STAYING ALIVE

A Sound Defense

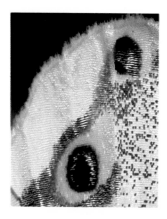

Fringed wing edges (above) muffle the sounds of a moth's flight. A garden tiger moth's fluffy body (below) absorbs sounds and doesn't echo bats' sonar clearly.

Bats and moths have been waging a kind of biological warfare for millions of years—an evolutionary competition resembling the response and counter-response of unfriendly nations as they develop new weapons.

Insect-eating bats have marvelous sonar systems that allow them to find moths and other insects on the wing at night. Some of the nocturnal moths they prey upon have equally clever devices for escaping.

To find their way in the dark and to locate prey, bats make high-pitched clicks that most humans can't hear. First the bats send out anywhere from 10 to 200 clicking signals a second. Then they measure, among other things, the time it takes the clicks to bounce off something solid and return to their highly sensitive ears. A bat's sonar is so accurate that the bat can avoid even small obstacles and home in on tasty moths.

The moths are not defenseless, however. Some of them have ingenious ways to escape detection by the bat's sonar or even to turn the sonar to their own advantage. First of all, these moths can hear a bat's clicks by means of tiny ears on the sides of their bodies. Sensitive to the direction and volume of sounds, the ears register where the bat is coming from and how far away it is.

A moth's ears pick up a bat's signals as they strike the moth, before the bat receives any telltale echoes. A moth can hear a bat coming from 100 feet away. The bat, however, has to be within 12 feet of the moth before it knows the moth is there. Having that margin of nearly 90 feet gives the slower moth time to change course before being identified and to get away, maybe.

Just how the moth changes its course

depends on where the bat is. Experiments show that if the incoming sound is weak, indicating that the bat is far away, the moth makes a beeline out of the vicinity, flying straight away from the sound. In this configuration, the moth's body presents the smallest area to the bat, minimizing the likelihood of sending an echo back. The bat may never detect the moth.

Stronger clicks indicate that a bat is probably zeroing in on the moth, and they prompt the moth to take extreme evasive action: tight turns and erratic loops and dives. It may even fold its wings and drop straight to the ground to avoid its pursuer. Erratic flight is an effective defense because, since the bat's sonar sends out only intermittent clicks, it does not have a continuous "picture" of its prey. It must choose its course on the basis of a series of "fixes." By moving unpredictably, the moth gives the bat no clue as to where it will be next.

Sensitive ears and evasive tactics are not the moth's only defenses. Their soft, fluffy bodies partially absorb a bat's signals, muffling the echoes just as rugs muffle the sounds in a room. And some moths fly almost noiselessly, a technique useful for anything hunted by predators with keen ears. After all, bats might hear the flutter of moths' wings as well as the echoes of their own sonar.

Some moths are even equipped with their own ultrasonic defense, high-pitched noises made by tiny clickers on their third pair of legs. Upon hearing a bat, these moths start making clicks in the range that the bat can hear—short bursts of several thousand clicks a second. These signals advertise the moth's presence, a seemingly suicidal act that really is a super defense. Some of the moths that make these clicks are distasteful, and bats soon learn not to eat them. And, as often happens in nature, mimicry comes into play, too: Some tasty moths send out bogus warnings of unpleasantness, cashing in on the bats' previous experiences with the unpalatable sort. Thus, the battle wages on, with neither side gaining superiority. Caught up in a war with no certain victor or loser, these creatures are a testimony to nature's balance of powers.

With thin eardrums (1) located in their thoraxes, some moths can hear the high-pitched sonar of a bat hunting for prey. The moths respond by flexing their hind legs to bend stiff clickers (2) and send out ultrasonic sounds of their own. The bat associates these clicks with moths that aren't very good to eat and heads for happier hunting grounds.

STAYING ALIVE

The Great Pretenders

Bluffers all, these creatures defend themselves by looking dangerous. The crucifix toad (above) inflates its body to intimidate an enemy. The hickory horned devil sports harmless horns (right). The frilled lizard (opposite) erects its cape to appear ferocious. It is a fake, nonetheless; it would rather flee than fight.

A poker player need not have a handful of aces to come out a winner. He need not even have a winning hand—provided he is an excellent bluffer. Some of the creatures not dealt aces in nature's game of defense use a similar strategy for coming out ahead. Although given few weapons to use against predators, they have the ability to bluff their way out of precarious situations by appearing far more fierce and dangerous than they really are.

One basic strategy: Look as large as possible. The hognose snake, perhaps best known for playing dead in defense, also has an inflating trick. When threatened, it sometimes swells to twice its normal width—earning the nickname "puff-adder." Some frogs and toads also accomplish this by gulping great amounts of air so that their bodies inflate like balloons. Their fattened bodies may even prevent some snakes from swallowing them.

Another striking creature, the frilled lizard of Australia and New Guinea, has a bark immeasurably worse than its bite. When threatened, it opens its mouth wide and fans out flaps of skin around its throat, thus appearing much larger than it is. The lizard enhances its act by hissing, rearing on its hind legs, and angrily thrashing its tail. But for all its appearance as a menacing dragon, it has only one real form of self-protection: If it fails to impress its provoker, it turns tail and runs away as fast as it can.

Another beast that makes the most of its decidedly nasty looks is the hickory horned devil, a five-inch-long caterpillar with menacing orange spikes curving from its body. It, too, is completely harmless, although its disguise could easily fool predators—and curious humans.

A more elaborate survival strategy can be found in another group of great pretenders, the coral snakes. Over 70 species of snakes in North and South America have similar combinations of white, yellow, black, or red "coral" bands. Though the true coral snakes are highly poisonous, the so-called false

coral snakes — members of another family — are harmless or only mildly poisonous. Clearly, mimicry is going on here — but who is mimicking whom?

Amazingly, it appears that both the highly poisonous and the harmless snakes are the ones that benefit by copying the mildly poisonous one. Why? Because that is the snake most likely to have taught its predators a lesson — leave banded snakes alone! The highly poisonous coral snake would simply kill off predators, and the harmless snake would, of course, leave them unharmed. Only the mildly poisonous snake leaves its attackers with a painful memory and a subsequent prejudice against eating any coral banded snakes.

Even though the highly poisonous snake is the best prepared for deadly competition, it is the mildly poisonous snake that has the key to fixing future games. Of course, competition in nature is no amateur sport; winning is the only aim. But the secret, as ever, lies in how the game is played.

Fighting Back

The camouflaged scorpionfish (left) and frightened hedgehog (right) have something in common: defensive spines that make an attacker feel attacked. The scorpionfish's needle-shaped spines on its back are grooved tubes with poison glands at their bases. The hedgehog's sharp spines aren't poisonous, but they cover most of its body. When threatened, the animal coils into a tight ball until danger is past.

When chess players say "the best defense is a good offense," they merely parrot a lesson proved innumerable times in nature. Every major animal group has some species that repel would-be predators with body structures that are virtually offensive weapons—from the surgeonfish's blade near its tail and the porcupine's familiar quills to an adhesive slime that some salamanders use to glue shut the mouths of hungry snakes.

Many of these animals that take the offense to defend themselves rely on stabbing weapons. Almost all the scorpionfish have highly adapted dorsal fins featuring rows of grooved spines that squirt venom into the puncture wounds they create. Glands at the base of each spine store the strongest poison of any fish in the sea. When another fish attacks the scorpionfish and gets stabbed by a spine, it almost assuredly dies. For man, punctures from Caribbean scorpionfish are very painful; wounds from some Indo-Pacific species can be fatal.

Adding to their menace, these ugly customers often blend so well with their surroundings that they virtually disappear from sight. Many can change their color to match their background, and some remain so sedentary that marine plants grow all over them, adding to their concealment.

Less fearsome by far are the hedgehogs of Europe, Asia, and Africa whose innumerable spines are not venomous. Nonetheless, they are formidable. These spines—inch-long hollow hairs braced on the inside for strength—are so sharp that 19th century German anatomists used them as pins in laying out dissections. Besides being sharp, the spines didn't corrode in the preservatives as metal pins did.

The hedgehog is so well protected that it need not bother to be cautious as it wad-

Fighting Back

dles through life. When the hedgehog is challenged or threatened, a long muscle encircling its abdomen contracts like a tightening drawstring to pull the hedgehog's spine-covered skin over its feet and head, protecting the naked belly. In this position, the little hedgehog is almost invulnerable.

At least two other land creatures, both rodents, share a prickly-skin defense with the hedgehogs. The Old World and the New World porcupines sport quill-covered bodies that protect these slow-moving animals from almost all predators.

Some quills are long and rigid. Others have moveable tips. Still others have bristly ends. The quills of New World species are barbed so that they easily penetrate an aggressor's flesh, but cannot be withdrawn without considerable pain and more tearing of the flesh. In fact, a porcupine quill, seemingly with a life of its own, will work its way deeper and deeper into the flesh, sometimes moving at a rate of one inch a day. If a quill works its way to a vital organ, it can kill.

In the ocean, too, there is a creature that can simultaneously erect many spines in defense. Pufferfish can blow themselves up like balloons by swallowing water or, if stranded on land, air. Normally the spines lie flat and smooth, but when a threatened fish inflates itself, the spines stand out like needles in a pincushion.

Usually the puffer's spiny appearance and sudden growth in size is enough to protect it from its enemies. But these fish also have an internal arsenal of toxic organs. In Japan, certain species of puffers are prepared and served as *fugu*, a potentially lethal delicacy. The chefs in certain restaurants are specially trained and licensed to remove the poison-containing organs, leaving just the tasty flesh. Most wild predators that eat an entire pufferfish without the benefit of such careful culinary preparation won't survive to bother the species again.

Among the sharpest defensive weapons in the animal world are the structures that lend the surgeonfish their peculiar name, their scalpels. On each side of a surgeonfish's body, just in front of the tail, is a specialized scale that is lethally sharp. In some of the Indo-Pacific species the flat blades are fixed in place, but in the surgeonfish of the Atlantic, the scalpels work like switchblades. They normally lie in grooves on the sides of the fish's body. When attacked, the fish erects the scalpels and slashes away with sweeps of its tail. Many an unaware fisherman has received nasty cuts while removing a surgeonfish from a net.

One of the cleverest self-defense systems occurs in some salamanders. The skin of these species secretes a substance that is toxic or so distasteful that predators avoid it and them. Besides being toxic to birds and some other predators, the secretions of one group of salamanders are so sticky they can glue parts of a garter snake's body together—including its jaws! In the struggle to swallow the salamander, the snake may coil

The surgeonfish (opposite) slashes predators with the yellow "scalpel" on each side of its body just in front of the tail. The well-named puffer (left) inflates itself and erects its spines when threatened. The salamander (below) secretes a milky slime worse than distasteful. It can cement a snake's mouth shut.

STAYING ALIVE

Fighting Back

A sea hare releases a defensive cloud of purple ink. A relative of clams and oysters, the sea hare has only a small, internal shell.

around its prey, smearing the salamander's slime all over itself. The slime quickly dries and turns into a tough glue, causing the snake to stick to itself for as long as two days. Alas, the snake is caught by its seemingly easy catch.

If it is impossible to stab, poison, or immobilize your enemy, it is time to make a getaway. And that is just what squid, octopuses, cuttlefish, and shell-less marine snails called sea hares do. Squid eject a puff of ink that resembles the shape of the squid, and the predator is likely to attack the inky ghost while the squid jets away. The brown ink ejected by octopuses and cuttlefish is thought to temporarily paralyze the sight and smell in some of their enemies. The sea hare produces an even lovelier screen of purplish, billowing ink that is truly a masterpiece in the art of self-defense.

Borrowed Weapons

Organisms that adapt have the greatest chances for long-term survival. For the day-to-day survival of a few select animals, adaptation takes the form of adoption — borrowing other creatures' weapons to build their own arsenals. Some adopt entire bodies as havens of safety; others borrow bits of bodies, poisonous pieces from other animals.

The brightly colored clownfish, for example, adopts the tangle of a sea anemone's poisonous mop of tentacles as its home. This toxic tangle is a lethal place for most fish because each anemone tentacle is armed with venomous stinging cells. Touch one and it shoots out a barbed harpoon laced with paralyzing poison. But one fish's hell is another fish's heaven, and the clownfish settles comfortably within the deadly swaying strands, gaining a measure of protection that its own body cannot give it.

Staking out a claim on the sanctuary, however, is not easy. The clownfish just setting up residence is as vulnerable to the stinging cells as any other ocean denizen, and coaxing an "acceptance" from the anemone can be a painful experience. The clownfish begins the relationship by boldly charging into the anemone's tentacles. The stinging cells shoot out their poison and the tentacles try to cling. The fish quickly jerks away. This underwater game of tag may continue for hours until, finally, the tentacles stop stinging.

Each time the little fish darts head-on into the tentacles, it coats parts of its body with the anemone's slime. This slime, which keeps the anemone's cells from stinging each other when they touch, also provides immunity to this special visitor. When its body is thoroughly coated with the protective slime, the clownfish can get to the business of housekeeping.

The anemone's guest register isn't signed by singles only. Sometimes couples settle in one anemone, laying their eggs at its base and raising their young there until the next generation is old enough to find its own home. Larger anemones may shelter several fish. But no matter how many live-in guests the anemone harbors, its tentacles act as guards to keep out trouble.

The partnership between fish and anemone, like any good relationship, is not one-sided. The fish gains protection, but it also serves its host well, luring potential food into the tentacles and even bringing meals home from its feeding forays. The territorial little fish will chase away any intruding members of its own kind. But more important for the anemone, its tenant fiercely defends its home against attacks from anemone-eating fish. The fish may even rid the tentacles of parasites.

Some hermit crabs don smaller, but none-

A Philippine tomato clownfish nestles within its deadly sea anemone home. The fish slowly builds enough immunity to the stinging cells to settle among them and borrow their protection. To repay its host, the clownfish attracts food to the anemone and fiercely attacks its enemies.

STAYING ALIVE

Borrowed Weapons

The "cowboy crab" of Hawaii, like a gun-toting Wild West hero, fends off its enemies by wielding a lethal sea anemone in each claw (top). A sea slug (opposite) dines on an animal equipped with stinging cells. The slug ingests these cells without triggering them, then transfers them to its white "horns." An attacker that bites the sea slug gets a mouthful of stinging cells.

theless potent, anemones atop their shells. The clownish headgear provides the crab with food, camouflage, and protection. A predator may think twice before messing with the hermit's poisonous attire.

Even more clever, the cowboy crab of the Indo-Pacific carries a stinging anemone in each claw, fending off adversaries like some two-gunned Wyatt Earp of the Old West. When an enemy comes close, the crab thrusts an anemone, or two, in its face. If a tasty morsel happens by, the crab may let the anemone do the work of catching it, and then steal the food for itself.

Like the cowboy crab, one kind of octopus adds to its defense by wielding stingers from another creature—the deadly tentacles of the Portuguese man-of-war. A marine biologist catching octopuses one night made the painful discovery. As he lifted a small female, he was stung on the arms—though he knew octopuses don't sting. Closer inspection showed that the octopus had stolen pieces of man-of-war tentacles and

had stuck the fragments in the suckers of its own grasping arms. Just how the octopus manages this without getting stung remains a mystery, but suction cups armed with stinging cells seem formidable weapons.

The man-of-war tentacles, sometimes streaming 30 feet into the ocean, contain masses of stinging cells. Designed to defend the man-of-war and to kill fish for its food, these tentacles can also cause excruciating pain to humans. Yet this murderous curtain provides a haven for another ocean creature, the aptly named man-of-war fish. This little fish, in fact, spends its entire life swimming within the business ends of the man-of-war's tentacles. Marked with silver and blue stripes that match the colors of the tentacles, the fish not only gains a weapon from the tentacles, it completely disappears among them.

The fish may attract prey for its host, dine on crumbs from its benefactor's table, and even take an occasional munch from a tentacle. Whether they abide there by invitation or stealth—science does not know—the little fish borrows weapons from its own potential predator for its own defense.

Some sea slugs, shell-less marine snails, borrow the stinging cells of other creatures in an intriguing way. These soft-bodied beauties browse in shallow tropical seas and coral reefs, eating relatives of anemones that also have stingers containing explosive barbs. Somehow, the stinging cells pass intact through the sea slug's digestive system. They neither harm the slug nor lose any of their ammunition. Then, as if by some conjurer's trick, the stinging cells end up at the tips of the horns that cover the sea slug's body. When an enemy of the seemingly defenseless sea slug tries to take a bite, it gets a mouthful of stinging cells.

And so these creatures given limited protection, or none at all, fend off their enemies by borrowing from nature's vast armament. Among animals, it seems, the line between the powerful and the defenseless is blurred by these borrowers of weapons.

4 POPULATING THE FUTURE

POPULATING
THE FUTURE

Finding The Better Half

blood vessels near the surface of the skin. The creation of the blue is a bit more complicated. Blue wavelengths in light striking the mandrill's skin are scattered by millions of tiny particles suspended in transparent cells—just as the blue wavelengths in sunlight are scattered by air molecules, creating the blue sky we see. That means of scattering light is called "Tyndall scattering," and most animals that are blue get their coloration the same way.

Another notably colorful creature is the male anole. This slender, green or brown lizard threatens competitors and lures potential mates by extending a bone in his neck that has a flap of brilliantly colored skin attached to it. The color of the dewlap identifies some lizard species. To guarantee species identification, the male anole squarely braces his front legs and does "push-ups," bobbing up and down at a rhythm unique to his species. The bobbing pattern is attractive only to females of his own kind.

Attractive coloration is widespread among birds, most of which secure their mates by flaunting brightly colored feathers. Often, only the males are conspicuously colored; females remain more protectively shaded to hide them while they nest. Feather colors come from three sources: pigments in the cells (similar to paints and dyes); Tyndall scattering (like that in the mandrill's skin); and light-wave interference. Examples of interference colors are the bright, iridescent hues of mallards, pheasants, and hummingbirds. The surface of these birds' feathers is covered by tiny, thin plates that make light behave in special ways. When light waves hit the plates, certain colors are reinforced and other colors cancelled out. The reinforced colors remain visible, and the cancelled colors disappear from sight.

The use of feathers for courtship reaches a high art in a family of spectacular birds, the birds of paradise. There are more than 40 species of these birds, each so beautiful that when Magellan first brought some to

Europe from their native New Guinea, the Spaniards said they came from Paradise.

Not only are the males colored and plumed in a most extraordinary manner, but also—to attract the attention of the more conservatively attired females—they display their flashy finery in a rakish way. Count Raggi's bird of paradise first dances about on a tree limb, throwing its plumes high and its wings upward. If a female shows any interest, the male then leans over until he is nearly upside down so that his feathers flash in the light more radiantly than ever.

More like the anole and the mandrill than like the bird of paradise, the male frigate bird uses a colorful patch of skin to repel competitors and attract mates. Inhabitants of tropical waters, these large sea birds often join terns and boobies in immense breeding colonies on islands. Like a bachelor getting ready to settle down, the male chooses a site and constructs a raggle-taggle nest of

The flashy bills of puffins (p. 143), the brightly colored dewlap of the anole (above), and the gaudy mask of the mandrill (opposite) are signals that attract the attention of the better half.

POPULATING THE FUTURE

Finding The Better Half

sticks. He then defends it from rivals and invites far-away females to come nearer by showing off his unique advertising sign — a huge, inflated, striking red sac on his throat. This natty pouch is nearly as large as he is. No nuptial slacker, the male puffs his pouch for hours at a time, even after mating. When his new mate has laid her egg, his brilliant sac fades to a dull orange, its sex-related role temporarily ended.

The animals that rely on bright colors to advertise for mates either live in areas of high visibility or have excellent vision. Animals living in woods or other habitats that make it difficult for them to spot one another use other ways to lure partners.

Many creatures use scent as their principal means of sexual communication, especially those that are active at night or are small and live relatively far apart. Interestingly, that gift is most highly developed in insects, particularly in moths. Most female moths attract mates by secreting substances called pheromones. A pheromone is so powerful that it can draw a male moth from miles away; only a few molecules need reach his highly sensitive antennae for him to detect the presence of a female. He locates her by flying in the direction of the scent.

For other animals, sound accomplishes the same function. It, too, can penetrate where sight cannot. Frogs and toads find their mates in crowded ponds by sounding distinctive mating calls. In some species, an inflatable sac — actually a continuation of the mouth's lining — increases the call's vol-

Having attracted a mate, a male frigate bird still inflates his throat sac to warn other males to stay away. The bird even inflates the sac during flight. Once the female lays her egg, however, the male stops showing off.

147

POPULATING THE FUTURE

Finding The Better Half

Using its resonant throat sac, a siamang gibbon fills the forest with booming cries. An entire family will sing together, warning others to keep their distance.

ume. The calls are so distinctive that in a few instances they are the only trait that identifies otherwise indistinguishable species.

Like frogs, some primates known for their booming calls have throat sacs that amplify sound. Among these are the siamang gibbons. At sunrise and sunset, they use their lusty voices to establish their home territory and to sing out—at times, some scientists believe, just because they feel good.

What is music to a male mosquito differs from species to species. The mosquito's highly sensitive system for hearing—the Johnston's organ, located at the base of each antenna—is tuned to perceive the sound created by a female's wingbeats. The frequency of the beats and the pitch of the sound make the difference. The male responds only to the tone of the females of his species. When his antennae are appropriately stimulated, he will fly toward the sound. Thus, a tuning fork vibrating at the same frequency as the "call" of a given species can attract a swarm of male mosquitoes eager to mate. And the unfortunate soprano who strikes and holds the right note may find a hoard of mosquitoes swarming towards her mouth.

The best known of serenading lovers are the birds. Although birds sing year-round, their songs become louder and livelier when they are looking for mates. Indeed, the association of song and courtship seems a natural one. Classically romantic settings for human beings, as well as for birds, seem always to feature music in the background.

Another romantic cliché makes a more unexpected appearance in the courtship of a different kind of animal. Before courting, snails of the *Helix* group circle each other. When they get close enough, each snail suddenly shoots a "love dart" into the body of its partner, inducing courtship behavior in the recipient—if the two are of the same species. While that erotic stab may not bring about romantic love in the usual sense, the dart of the *Helix* seems strikingly like the arrows from Cupid's bow.

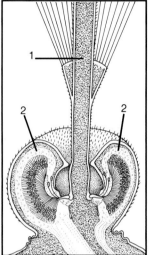

The croak of a frog and the hum of a mosquito carry the lure of sex. The male Fowler's toad (left) amplifies his call with an inflatable throat sac. In the male mosquito (above left) the sensitive Johnston's organ at the base of each antenna (above) monitors the antenna's vibrations. When the antennae vibrate at the same frequency as the wingbeats of a female of the same species, the male knows a mate is near. The direction in which the shafts of the antennae (1) vibrate stimulates nerves (2) in the Johnston's organ that tell the male which way to fly to find the female.

POPULATING THE FUTURE

Special Delivery

In the special-delivery mating of octopuses, the male (to the left here) displays the stripes of breeding. His *hectocotylus,* a tentacle adapted for sexual use, carries a capsule of sperm to the female. When the capsule is placed in the female's mantle (below), the sperm are released and fertilize her thousands of eggs.

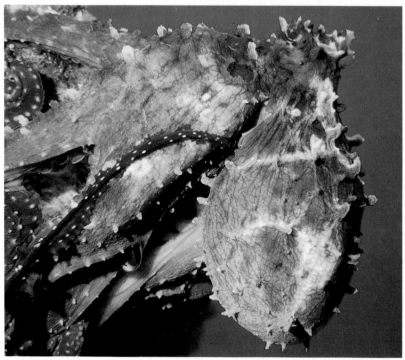

An embrace seems to be a required act in the etiquette of sexual encounters. There are, however, many creatures whose courtship and mating include no embraces. Males of one kind of fish shoot pointed sperm capsules into the skin of their partners; leeches load their sperm into mucus that dissolves the skin of their partners; and male argonauts, a type of octopus, leave part of the sperm-carrying arm inside the female. Though they may seem bizarre, these "special delivery" methods work just as well as those that involve tender proximity.

At first glance, a many-armed octopus would seem to be made for hearty embraces. Not so. The octopus's sucker-dotted tentacles are very effective for traveling and hunting. For mating, though, they only get in the way—all of them, that is, but one.

That one is the male tentacle known as the *hectocotylus,* specialized for sex. The male mates by placing the spoon-shaped tip

Golden silk spiders mate in the female's web. The much smaller male grasps the female to insert a leg-like palp carrying sperm.

of this arm into the female's mantle cavity and depositing sperm packets.

The packets of sperm reach the tip of the specialized arm by wending their way from the male's internal genitals via an aqueduct made of a fold of skin. A large male may have hundreds of sperm packets in storage at one time in a pouch surrounding parts of his reproductive organs.

In one species, the argonaut, the hectocotylus is wrenched from the male and left inside the female during the course of mating. Naturalists used to think that these limbs were parasitic worms found only in females.

As the female octopus releases her eggs from her ovaries, they are fertilized by the sperm in her mantle cavity. She then lays her fertilized eggs on long strings which she attaches to the walls of a rock crevice.

Male spiders also possess a kind of sex arm. The male's front pair of "arms" are technically known as *pedipalps* ("touching arms"), or *palps* for short. It is the tips of these palps that are modified for sexual use.

The male spider of many species prepares for mating by spinning a small "sperm web." Hanging upside down, he presses his abdomen against his web until a sperm drop appears at his genital opening. Dipping his two palps into the liquid, he fills a reservoir at the tip of each palp.

The tips are usually dotted with tiny protrusions arranged in different patterns in different species. During mating, the protrusions become a kind of "key" that fits only into the "lock" of a female of the same kind.

The female spider's occasional cannibalistic behavior toward males has given her bad press. Typical mating is, however, tranquil. The male entwines with the female, places his palps in her genital opening, releases his sperm, and goes on his way. Even the black widow spider does not always live up to her name by killing her partner after mating. What does happen regularly, though, is that the tip of the male's palp breaks off during mating. When this happens, neither male nor female can ever mate again.

POPULATING THE FUTURE

Novel Nurseries

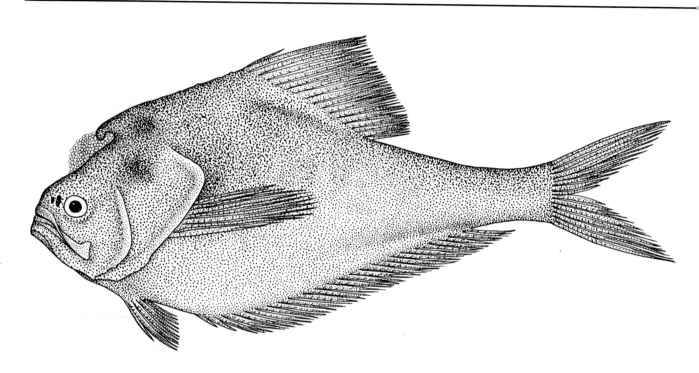

very concerned guardian. Several males gather around the eggs laid by a single female and stay with them for up to 20 days until the embryos start to move. Then each male takes between five and fifteen of the embryos on his tongue and slips them into his large vocal pouch. The tadpoles hatch and metamorphose into frogs, all within the safety of papa's vocal pouch.

While his charges are growing within him, the adult *vaquero* has no problem eating. But the tadpoles' increasing weight and size put tremendous pressure on the father's internal organs, and his shoulder bones are even shifted by the weight. When his wards are fully developed, papa merely opens his mouth and the young *vaqueros* jump out pell-mell, ready to start life on their own.

Marsupial frogs of South America also incubate their eggs within their bodies—in brood pouches on the females' lower backs. When ready to lay her eggs, the female puts her head low to the ground and raises her rear. A male frog clutching her shoulders

fertilizes the eggs as they pass under him. After the eggs enter the pouch, it closes after them. When the young become tadpoles, mother frog reaches up with her longest toe and pulls open her enlarged pouch. The young emerge to finish their development in nearby puddles.

An Australian frog has one of the strangest internal nurseries of all—the mother's stomach. The frog probably swallows her eggs shortly after they have been fertilized by a male. In her stomach, the young live off their yolk sacs for the duration, but mama cannot eat at all. Somehow her digestive system closes down to protect her young from being digested while they are in residence. Besides, there is simply no room for food in the stomach, with all the brood.

Forehead brooder fish of Australia and Asia leave egg-tending to the males. In maturing males, spines of the dorsal fin develop into a bony hook over the brow. Evidently, the female brooder lays her eggs on plants where they are fertilized by the male.

The male forehead brooder gets his name from his habit of carrying eggs on his brow. Apparently the female lays the eggs on underwater vegetation where they are fertilized. Then the male secures them to the hook on his forehead with their own entangling strands.

154

Before seeing the world from the safety of its mother's back, a baby koala spends six months inside her pouch.

POPULATING THE FUTURE

Novel Nurseries

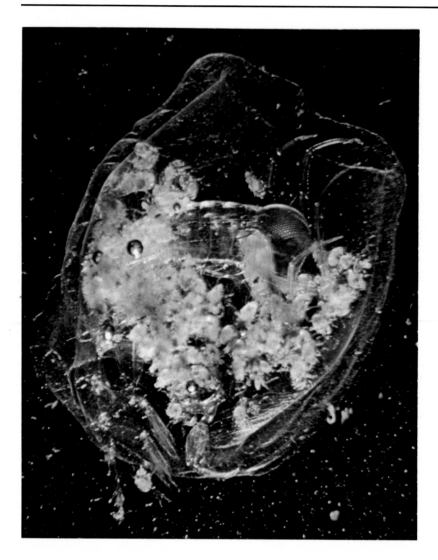

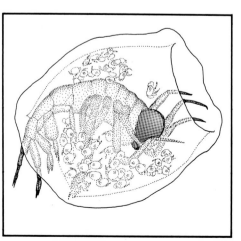

A many-legged *Phronima* anchors herself and her brood inside the transparent shell of an organism she has just eaten. She propels her stolen "baby buggy" by kicking with two hind feet that stick out of the shell at the bottom.

He then scoops up two clusters of eggs with his forehead hook and attaches one on each side of it. Sticky threads on the eggs themselves keep them secure on the fish's forehead until their time comes to hatch.

The argonaut, a close relative of the octopus, cares for her young with the aid of a shell. A pair of her arms secrete the paper-thin shell that she holds around her body. She lays her eggs in the shell and transports them there until they hatch. If threatened, she may retreat fully into the shell with them. Because of the fragility of this dainty, pearly shell, large unbroken specimens are highly prized by shell collectors.

Just as the argonaut's papery shell serves as an ideal nursery for her young, a koala mother's warm, soft pouch is the perfect nursery for her cuddly baby. Young koalas are born about one month after the parents mate and immediately scramble into their mother's pouch. Opening to the rear of the mother, this pouch will be the only home the baby koala will know for the next five to six months. At the end of this period, the young koala is strong enough and developed enough to leave the safety of its nursery.

A little oddity named *Phronima*, a simple invertebrate related to the shrimp, uses an aquatic baby buggy to carry her youngsters. The female first finds a barrel-shaped animal called a salp. She eats out the salp's insides but leaves its transparent shell. Climbing inside this barrel-shaped container, she lays several hundred eggs against the sides of the shell. Holding on with her forelegs, she uses her rear legs to swim. The young hatch by her side in the stolen buggy.

Some fish go to great lengths to protect their eggs. A species of tropical fish found in the Amazon lays its eggs out of the water on overhanging leaves. Male and female fish lock fins, leap out of the water, and cling to a leaf long enough to deposit a mass of fertilized eggs. Then, for days while the eggs incubate, the father keeps them wet by splashing water on them with his tail. Now that's a daring, caring parent.

An Egg-Laying Mammal

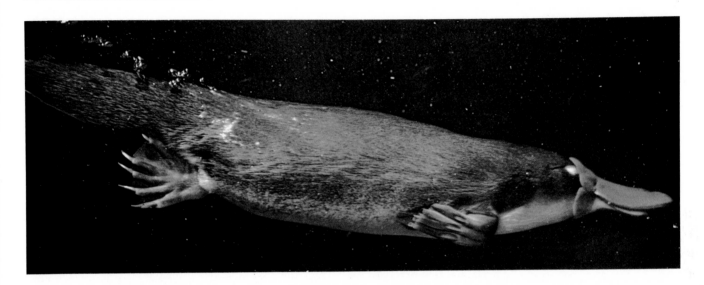

The question sounds as if it should be followed by a punch line: What has the bill and webbed feet of a duck, the flat tail of a beaver, lays eggs, and nurses its young? The question is no joke, but the answer is something undeniably funny-looking. It is the platypus—the "bits-and-pieces animal," as Australians call it.

The animal, in fact, seemed such an inconceivable mix of parts that when the first preserved specimen arrived in England from Australia in the early 1800's, scientists suspected a hoax and dismantled the pelt to uncover the presumed hidden stitches. As zoologists later discovered, however, the animal was genuine, an oddity whose body seems placed in an evolutionary no-man's-land between reptiles and mammals.

Although now classified as a mammal because it has fur and produces milk, the platypus has many reptilian traits. And while the animal has proved difficult to study because of its shyness in the wild and the difficulty of keeping it alive in laboratories, scientists welcome the challenge, for they believe the platypus may encapsulate the evolutionary history of some important mammalian features, live birth in particular.

Like its exterior, the platypus's reproductive anatomy is an apparent jumble of parts.

The female has only one functioning ovary —on the left side of her body—which is also true of female birds. And the male—like reptiles but unlike most mammals—has internal testicles housed within his body rather than descending from it.

Although the platypus lays leathery eggs as reptiles do, the development of its two eggs is more akin to that of mammalian embryos: They *grow* as they pass through the mother's body. Less than an eighth of an inch wide at first, they are five times that large when they are laid. The embryonic platypus also does not rely entirely on the egg's yolk for nutrients, as does a reptilian embryo, but absorbs some directly from the oviduct down which it travels. In that respect, it's something like the young of mammals nourished through placentas.

When the two eggs are laid, the mother curls around them in a nest of damp leaves, rarely leaving them until they hatch some two weeks later. Then—almost, but not entirely like other mammals—she nurses them with milk. The difference is that she has no nipples. The milk instead seeps out of pores on her abdomen, a process that provides scientists with yet another likely glimpse of the past—a clue to the ways modern mammals may have developed from reptiles.

Living link to the past, the platypus is an intriguing puzzle to scientists. They believe it may provide information about the evolutionary steps from reptiles to mammals. Its unique reproductive system combines characteristics of both.

POPULATING
THE FUTURE

Running
Against Time

With a warm spell and a heavy rain, Couch's spadefoot toads come out of hiding to find mates. Their harsh mating cries sound almost like the bleat of a goat or a sheep.

So much to do and so little time to do it. This human complaint is surprisingly true for some animals as well. Animals generally breed, or at least bear young, in the spring. That gives their offspring the long, food-rich summer months to grow strong to survive their first winter. But certain creatures that live in difficult environments must speed up their reproductive process to give their young the gift of life.

Prize-winners in the race against time are probably the spadefoot toads of the American Southwest. In barely two weeks, these amphibians mate, and their tadpoles hatch and metamorphose into little toads.

The two-inch-long spadefoot toads are distinguished by an adaptation that gives them their common name: a sharp-edged "spade" on the inside of each hind foot. The spade is made of keratin, the same as human fingernails.

What prompts such a rushed life style,

especially short when compared with the three to twelve months it takes most toads and frogs to go from egg to tadpole to adult?

Consider where many of these toads live: Arizona, New Mexico, western Texas, southern California—all regions with some of the lowest recorded rainfalls in the country. Yet, like the toads in wetter areas, the spadefoots must have a good puddle of water in which to mate and leave their eggs to develop.

During the long, rainless spells—weeks or even months in some places—the spadefoot uses its spade to burrow underground in search of moist soil where it can hide. But come a warm evening after a good, heavy rain and the once-dead, dried-out ponds burst into life with the toads' harsh cries. In the coolness of evening, first one male, then another, and another, sends out the distinctive call, a sound that can carry two miles or more over the flat landscape.

In response, the females join the group.

The louder the males call, the more the females are drawn to them. In short order, the pool becomes a bubbling, splashing mass of toad life. A male grabs the first toad he comes to. If the partner gives out a croak, that means it's a male also—so there's nothing doing there. The first male keeps up his search until at last he grasps a silent frog: a female for mating.

Even now, there is no time to waste. Before the night is out, many fertile eggs have been anchored to underwater greenery. The entire egg-laying session may be over in just two nights. As the last of the eggs are being laid, some of the first ones are already hatching into tiny tadpoles.

And all the time that the mating, egg-laying, and growing are going on, the pond is slowly drying up. If the tadpoles are to become adult toads, however, they need anywhere from two to nearly six weeks, depending on their species and on how much food they can get from the water in their pool. The less food they get, the longer it takes them to develop. Some spadefoot tadpoles gather at the bottom of the puddle, communally stirring up whatever food has settled there.

Still, the pool gets shallower and shallower. Soon the tadpoles may be left quite literally high and dry. If conditions become this severe, the tadpoles will school again, this time using their tails to swirl the water around and scoop out a small cavity in the bottom of the pool. With luck, the last of the water will settle in this hollow just long enough for the tadpoles to mature.

Should the worst happen—the pond dry up and all the tadpoles die—all is not lost. At the next rain, more toads may use the pond for mating and laying eggs. Then the remains of the tadpoles that didn't make it will provide a new generation with the nourishment it needs to beat the clock.

Far to the north of the spadefoot toads, farther north than any other reptile in North America is ever found, the red-sided garter snakes of western Canada run their own

After spadefoots mate, it's a race against time for the eggs to turn into tadpoles and the tadpoles into toads before their pool of water dries up. In less than two weeks, eggs can turn into tiny toadlets nearly one-half inch long.

POPULATING THE FUTURE

Running Against Time

Moist soil is home to a Couch's spadefoot toad (left), which digs its burrow with a sharp "spade" on each hind foot. For the red-sided garter snakes of western Canada, home is a cavern where they can wait out cold weather until the warmth of spring brings them out to mate (right).

race, not against heat and dryness but against cold. They must follow a rigid schedule to emerge from their cold-weather dens, mate, migrate, feed, give birth, and return to hibernation before the three short months of warm weather run out.

Being cold-blooded, the snakes are active only during warm weather. During the rest of the year, when winter temperatures may drop to 40 degrees below zero, the snakes gather in underground caverns—as many as 10,000 snakes in one den.

With the onset of warm weather, thousands of snakes pour forth from the dens. At first, almost all of the snakes are males. That way, when the females emerge later, immediate mating is virtually certain for them. After all, there is no time to waste. In another time-saving adaptation, the males' sperm are active immediately, having developed the previous summer.

In a tangle perhaps 100 snakes thick, the males crawl over each other to reach a female. They are driven to a mating frenzy by a special chemical she gives off called a *pheromone*—a general term used to refer

to a chemical one animal emits that affects the behavior of another. The female also avoids delays here by using pheromone she produced the previous summer.

In this so-called "mating ball," when one of the males successfully fertilizes a female, he deposits in her a jellylike plug that physically prevents other males from mating with her. At the same time, the male adds to the plug a pheromone of his own that makes the female unattractive to the other males. Now, without the pursuit of the males to delay her, the female slithers quickly away from the den, traveling as much as ten miles to the summer feeding grounds.

The act of mating induces the development of the female's eggs and the expulsion of any sperm left from last year's mating. By storing the new sperm until her eggs are ready to be fertilized six to eight weeks later, the female can travel without the burden of young growing inside her. At last the rush seems to be over. She will stay on the feeding grounds and give birth to more than 30 young before returning to the den in time for the next cold season's hibernation.

POPULATING
THE FUTURE

A Scarcity Of Mates

Populating the future is the biological bottom line, the show that must go on no matter what. If there are not enough mates to go around, then the standard script must be changed. Some species solve the problem by doing without mating. Others include organs of both sexes in their bodies.

Those species that perpetuate themselves without mating are called *parthenogenetic*. This method is common among primitive animals, but among vertebrates it is a talent limited nearly exclusively to the lizards.

Among the whiptail lizards, 13 species reproduce parthenogenetically. Each and every one of these lizards is a female, since each individual is a clone of her mother. How can a female reproduce without mating? Each of her eggs contains the full genetic inventory, in contrast to the eggs of sexual creatures, which contain only half the required genetic material and so must unite with sperm carrying the other half.

For years, scientists puzzled over parthenogenesis. It seemed as if none of its advantages justified the overwhelming disadvantage: the inability of the species to adapt to environmental changes, since every female is stamped from the same mold as her mother. The current assessment is that most parthenogenetic species live in small populations where environmental conditions are difficult. A search for mates and a complex mating ritual would consume too much time and energy there, so cloning may be the ticket for success, just as a factory cranking out many inexpensive copies of a single saleable item assures profits.

Under different conditions, different problems in finding a mate arise, so different solutions follow. Small, immobile creatures can suffer from a scarcity of mates even when one is only a few inches away. Some animals solve this problem by possessing both male and female sex organs within each individual. They are *hermaphrodites* (a term merging the names of Hermes and Aphrodite, Greek gods of male and female beauty). Even among hermaphrodites con-

This New Mexico whiptail lizard (opposite) need not bother to find a mate. The eggs in her body don't require fertilization in order to develop; she merely produces carbon copies of herself. The sea hares (right) play double or nothing when they find a mate. They are hermaphrodites, each having both male and female organs. By exchanging sperm, each fertilizes the eggs of the other.

siderable variety exists. Individuals may fertilize their own eggs or they may trade sperm, each fertilizing the eggs of another. In other species, eggs and sperm may mature separately so that an individual functions as male or female at different stages.

One of the latter type is the slipper limpet, a marine snail that lives stacked up in piles of eight to twelve individuals, with the oldest at the bottom. A slipper limpet begins life as a free-swimming larva seeking another limpet to alight upon. Once settled, it develops into a male and fertilizes the eggs of the mature females beneath him. Larvae

arriving later will attach to him, but he remains a male until the females beneath him die. Then slowly he turns female.

Sea hares, colorful shell-less relatives of the slipper limpets, differ from them in that each snail is simultaneously male and female. They link up into chains or even rings, with each sea hare being a male to the one in front and a female to the one behind. Each sea hare then produces up to 4,000,000 fertilized eggs that season. Few of them will survive, however, and the new generation of sea hares will once again have to deal with a scarcity of mates.

POPULATING
THE FUTURE

The Milky Way

The white-tailed deer (left) and the Dall sheep (above) are born with the grazers' four-chambered stomach, but they need only one chamber to digest their mothers' milk. Salts in the milk trigger the formation of a throat tube that leads directly into the fourth chamber.

Nothing looks complicated about the gentle tableau of a nursing fawn or Dall lamb. But the simple act of nursing is far more complex for a newborn grazing animal than for animals without the grazer's special digestive equipment: a four-chambered stomach.

The complex stomach is designed for breaking down the fibrous parts of a grazer's grassy food. And although a baby ruminant is born with the chambered stomach, it does not need all that sophisticated equipment to digest its mother's milk. So a system has evolved that enables the milk to bypass three of the four chambers.

Salts in the milk stimulate a nerve in the baby's mouth. That nerve causes a groove in the esophagus to contract so that it forms a tube that takes the milk directly into the fourth chamber. There, the milk is broken down, and the young ruminant soaks up the nutrition its body needs.

Good nutrition is the difference between life and death for a young ruminant. Fortunately for the newborn baby, its mother's first milk, a thick, yellow substance called *colostrum*, is packed full of antibodies against disease. These antibody molecules are too large to reach the developing young through the placenta; and, soon after birth, the walls of the digestive tract will not let them through either. The nursing ruminant has hardly more than a day to build its body's defenses through its mother's milk.

Suckling fawns, lambs, and other ruminants gain about one-tenth of their birth weight each day for the first week of their lives. That gain is vital for a young one who must follow its mother soon after birth.

A nursing fawn or lamb appears to receive affection as well as milk. And it does. Nursing forms a bond that keeps mother and baby together as the newborn learns to negotiate the dangerous path to independence.

BEYOND WILD EXPECTATIONS

The Wonderful Net

Fire and ice: Each is an appropriate part of a scenario for the end of the world — from the point of view of a human being, that is. While the equally burning sensations of scorching and freezing flesh are among the most painful experiences humans can imagine, intense cold and intense heat are the everyday conditions in which many animals live comfortably.

The nearly hairless walrus and the furred polar bear swim for hours in icy waters that would kill a human in minutes. A gull with its unprotected feet can stand imperturbably on ice. These animals can take the cold in part because of the insulating layers of fat, fur, or down and feathers that arctic explorers imitate with their felt-lined boots and down-filled parkas. But the animals also

have unseen advantages that no person can copy, though every visitor to a cold climate might wish to.

One advantage is their limbs' ability to withstand extreme cold. The feet of the gull standing on ice are probably just barely above freezing. The lower legs of caribou and other mammals of the Arctic also become nearly as cold as the ground they walk on. So far as is known, these animals feel no discomfort in their limbs; they certainly don't lose any mobility from the cold, as humans do. The gull and the caribou move about as nimbly on winter's ice and snow as they do on summer's dry land.

Another hidden advantage comes from a system of specially arranged arteries and veins that prevent the cold blood which returns from an animal's extremities—its legs, flippers, or tail, for example—from dangerously lowering the temperature of the rest of the body. This surprisingly simple yet highly beneficial system is known as the "wonderful net."

The principle behind the "net" is familiar to engineers: Heat released by pipes carrying hot water or steam in one direction is used to warm adjacent pipes carrying cool water in the opposite direction.

In animals that have "nets," arteries function as the hot pipes. They carry warm blood from the heart to the body's poorly insulated extremities where heat is quickly dissipated. The veins are like the cool pipes. They carry cooled blood back to the heart. When a warm artery lies parallel to or is surrounded by cool veins, the warmth escaping the artery heats the cool blood in the veins. In that way, the wonderful net prevents the heat in the arteries from being wasted, saving it instead to keep the vital internal organs warm.

The walrus's wonderful nets are located where its flippers join its body. The nets leave just enough warmth in the arterial blood to keep the flippers functional. In the

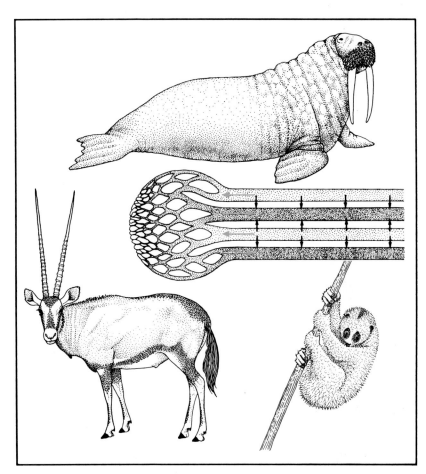

gull, the nets are located in the body just above where it joins the legs. While the nets control what otherwise would be a tremendous loss of heat from the bird's naked legs, they also safeguard the bird's feet. By keeping them just above freezing, the nets prevent the feet from melting their icy perch. Otherwise, the melted ice could refreeze, making the bird a prisoner.

Arctic animals are not the only ones that need protection from the cold. Because water is so efficient at stealing heat from the body, even creatures that inhabit temperate seas need some protection. Likewise, some animals that inhabit tropical forests are highly sensitive to coolness.

The manatee is a large, gentle mammal that lives in the warm coastal waters of the

The "wonderful net" is a miraculous bit of biological engineering by which arteries going to the extremities (light areas) exchange heat or gases with returning veins (dark areas). The net can conserve heat, as it does in the walrus; remove excess heat, as it does in the long-horned oryx, a desert dweller; and aid in the exchange of gases, as it does in the limbs of the slow loris.

BEYOND WILD EXPECTATIONS

The Wonderful Net

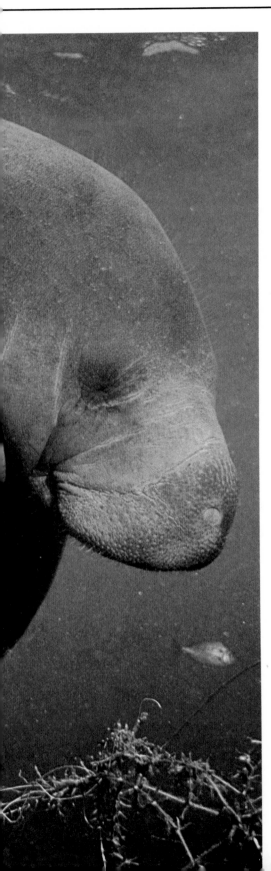

Atlantic. The manatee has a net between its flippers and body to prevent the water from spiriting away too much body heat from the broad surface of the flippers.

In jungles farther south lives the two-toed sloth, a creature that spends most of its life hanging lethargically upside down from tree branches. The sloth's inactivity makes maintaining a stable body temperature difficult. Despite its fur, the sloth is so sensitive to cool air that it shivers when the temperature drops to 80 degrees, as it often does at night. Wonderful nets between its limbs and its body help retain valuable heat, keeping the body comfortable.

While most fish lose great quantities of heat to water passing through their gills, several types of tuna, sharks, and a few other fish have nets that reduce such losses. The resulting body warmth permits the muscles to contract and relax more quickly, making these fish among the fastest swimmers. Some tuna reach speeds exceeding 40 miles an hour for short bursts.

For some creatures, the net becomes too much of a good thing during strenuous

Even animals of gentle climates need protection from the cold. Temperate waters rob heat from the warm-blooded manatee (opposite); cool tropical nights steal warmth from the sloth (above). Wonderful nets in both animals allow the temperature of their limbs to fall below that of their bodies to conserve heat.

BEYOND WILD EXPECTATIONS

The Wonderful Net

activity when they actually need to dissipate excess body heat. In many creatures, the cool blood returning from the extremities can be shunted away from the outgoing arteries. The arterial blood thus flows uncooled to the extremities, where its heat is lost to the cooler air. That is one way that seals, for example, keep from overheating when moving about on land.

In seals and similar animals, the net must be bypassed to cool the body. In other creatures, the net itself is a cooling device. These animals have a wonderful net at the base of their brain to prevent excess body heat from reaching it, since a rise of only a few degrees can damage this delicate organ. This net works a little differently than the ones in a seal. Blood returning from the brain to the heart passes through the moist nasal cavity where evaporation cools it. Panting increases evaporation and lowers the blood's temperature even more. Cooled nasal blood then flows to the base of the brain where the veins form a net with the brain-destined arteries. The warm arteries lose some of their heat to the cooler veins, and so keep the temperature of the brain several degrees lower than that of the rest of the body. This net enables desert mammals like oryxes to survive intense heat without brain damage.

The wonderful net also helps prevent dehydration. Most animals protect their brains by cooling their whole bodies through sweating or panting, losing a great deal of water in the process. A person, for example, can sweat as much as three gallons in one day. Water losses of this magnitude would be extremely dangerous to a desert animal such as the oryx, which has little access to water. The oryx, therefore, prevents water loss by slowing its metabolism to reduce the amount of heat its body produces and by allowing its body temperature to rise during the hottest period of the day. That reduces its need to sweat or pant. The oryx's brain remains shielded from this elevated temperature by the net nestled at its base.

The net has several other specialized functions that are unrelated to body temperature. In some fish, it helps maintain the gas content of the swim bladder—the internal sac that gives fish their buoyancy—by exchanging gases rather than heat. And in the slow loris, a small tree-dwelling primate of Africa and Southeast Asia, the wonderful net aids the exchange of oxygen and carbon dioxide in the muscles used to grip tree branches, thus making the muscles less subject to fatigue. Like a safety net of rope, these wonderful nets have many uses, all in vital service to those fortunate enough to have them.

A wonderful net in its head keeps the oryx's brain cool in the sun's scorching heat (opposite). In the slow loris of Malaysia, the net aids the exchange of oxygen and carbon dioxide in muscles used to grip tree branches (above). The slow loris can hang for hours without any fatigue.

BEYOND WILD EXPECTATIONS

Three-Layered Parka

smaller flippers because excess heat is more easily eliminated in the antarctic chill.

For all its appearance as a clumsy, over-dressed comic on land, the penguin is a streamlined flier once it enters the water. Indeed, it does "fly" through the water, flapping its narrow, pointed flippers, really modified wings. Heavily muscled, the flippers have only short feathers, which insulate without adding unnecessary drag to the flipper's movement through the water. As proof that the bird really is a flier, the penguin has the same large breastbone that aerial fliers have for attachment of powerful wing muscles. Truly flightless birds, such as the ostrich, have much smaller breastbones.

Unlike many swimming birds that use their webbed feet for paddling, the penguin uses its feet only for steering. With its head back against its shoulders and its feet pressed tight against its body (except when steering, of course), the penguin takes on a spindle-like shape that cuts through the water with a minimum of effort.

The effort required during swimming is further reduced by the penguin's bones, which are solid, not light and hollow like those of airborne birds. The extra weight

An emperor penguin cools off—its insulation is so efficient that on sunny days the bird may overheat. Outstretched flippers let cold air cool the hot blood circulating near the skin (above). When under water, a penguin's iris opens wide to gather light (right, top). When above water, the iris contracts (right, bottom), shielding the eye from the blinding glare of the ice.

helps the bird remain under water, enabling it to spend its energy chasing food rather than trying to remain submerged.

The swimming penguin reduces its buoyancy even further by compressing its feathers to force out the trapped air before submerging. It also exhales, leaving only enough air in its lungs to keep them inflated.

As a penguin swims, it may repeatedly jump clear of the water, going up and down like a roller coaster. This "porpoising" technique is thought to propel the bird the maximum distance for the least effort. Swimming under water takes two to five times less energy for the bird than swimming through surface waves. Yet, it must surface frequently to breathe. Porpoising lets it breathe without battling the turbulence at the surface.

The penguin not only moves better in water than on land, it also sees better. Other aquatic birds can flex their eyes' lenses to adjust the focus when going from air to water and back. A penguin lacks this ability, and its eyes focus best in water—where keen vision is crucial for finding food. As a result, the bird is as short-sighted in the air as a human is under water.

With such adaptations for cold, heat, and life under water, it's no wonder that penguins have spread from the South Pole to the equator. Of them all, however, those that live on the fringes of Antarctica survive conditions harsher than those met by any other bird. Be it ever so frosty, that continent of ice and snow is home, made comfortable by the versatile three-layered parka.

When traveling fast and not feeding, penguins sometimes rhythmically arch out of the water, an efficient form of swimming called *porpoising*.

BEYOND WILD EXPECTATIONS

A Collapsible Creature

A Weddell seal basks on the ice of its antarctic home. Weddells spend long hours under the sun, restoring to their muscles oxygen used during hour-long exploratory dives.

Antarctica: In terms of human comforts, no environment seems harsher. Bitter cold and near-total darkness jointly reign during its long winter. On land, double-digit readings below zero are the rule, and the sea's temperature drops below water's official freezing point. Yet the Weddell seal, a mammal as warm-blooded as ourselves, feels so at home there that it thrives and even gets fat during the harsh winter.

The seal's strategy might be stated this way: Since the land has the most cold and the least food in winter, take to the sea — for weeks at a stretch, or even longer. The water's temperature does not drop below 28 degrees, and the sea holds plenty of food, albeit sometimes 1,000 feet or more down.

Working from the outside in, the Weddell seal's first asset for coping with freezing temperatures is a three-inch layer of insulating blubber. The Weddell's sparse coat of stiff guard hairs does little to protect it against

the cold, but the blubber does the trick. Falling snow does not even melt on the seal's well-insulated body.

Keeping its body warm, however, is only half the story of the seal's antarctic success. To eat, it must dive deep under the ice for long periods of time to catch the deep-swimming fish, squid, and crustaceans that make up its diet. Indeed, a Weddell seal can dive down to 2,000 feet, travel more than a mile in a single dive, and stay submerged for up to an hour. For the air-breathing seal, this means coping with two critical problems: a limited oxygen supply and the tremendous pressure of the water.

A Weddell seal has half again as much blood as terrestrial mammals its size. This extra blood means extra oxygen for the seal on its deep-sea dives. As the seal goes under, its heartbeat slows to about one-tenth its normal rate. The slower the heart beats, the slower the blood circulates, and the longer the oxygen lasts. The seal's muscles, too, can function without a continuous oxygen supply, so the blood and its precious oxygen cargo can safely be shunted to the heart and brain.

To cope with the tremendous pressure of the water during a deep dive and with the danger of decompression when resurfacing, the seal uses a deceptively simple solution: It yields to the pressure. Just before going under, a seal breathes out, reducing the amount of air it carries in its lungs. As it descends — at speeds of nearly 400 feet a minute — its flexible rib cage collapses with the increased pressure, pushing the air out of the lungs and into the trachea. The trachea, too, is designed to collapse under pressure. Unlike a human's round windpipe, a seal's is oval, so that its walls can compress easily.

A scuba diver who surfaces too quickly will be overcome by "the bends," a sometimes fatal nitrogen poisoning of the blood caused by breathing air under pressure. But when the seal's lungs collapse, air is pushed into rigid airways where gas exchange does not occur. The nitrogen in the air cannot enter the blood, and the seal can resurface quickly without any danger.

Having found ways to survive in the cold water and to dive to depths where its food can be found, the Weddell seal must still manage to breathe while beneath thick ice. It does this by chiseling holes in the ice around its neighborhood. If a breathing hole freezes over, the seal chisels it open again. Here another adaptation comes into play. The Weddell seal's upper front teeth point forward and serve as ice-boring tools.

The Weddell seals with all their trappings survive where no other mammals can: under the ice. They fear nothing, not even the occasional scientist who may briefly invade their icy kingdom, so long have they reigned alone and untouched in the cold.

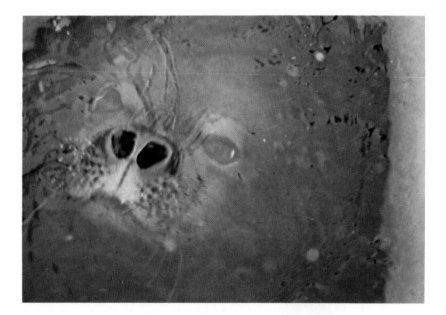

A Weddell seal pokes through one of the breathing holes it maintains in the ice (top). When a hole freezes over, the seal reams it out from below with protruding front teeth. Though they swim under the ice for distances of a mile or more, the seals return to the same breathing holes again and again (bottom). They may use sight or sonar to find their way.

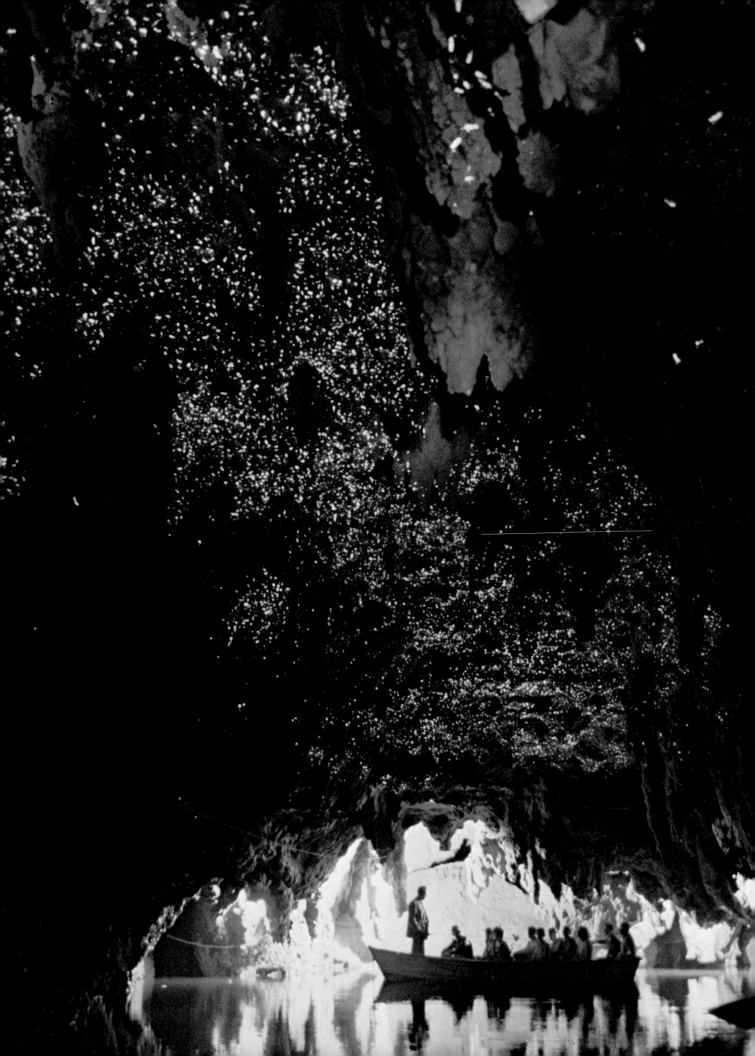

BEYOND WILD EXPECTATIONS

Natural Lights

When a fuse blows and the lights go dark, a flashlight is a mighty handy thing to own, provided the batteries work. At night or in the dark deep of the sea, some insects and marine creatures use flashlights that come with lifetime guarantees. Indeed, the flashlights themselves guarantee life, for they repel enemies or attract meals and mates.

The smallest bioluminescent animals are tiny bacteria. They are permanently powered by a chemical that creates light when combined with oxygen. Most insects and sea creatures use a similar reaction to produce their light in special glands scattered over their bodies. Some fish and squids cheat, though, by keeping herds of the tiny bacteria in these glands. These exploiters control the glowing servants to suit their own purposes by adjusting the amount of oxygen available in the glands.

No matter which type, these living lights are extraordinarily efficient. Light bulbs typically radiate most of their energy as wasted heat—as much as 97 percent. In sharp contrast, some glowing insects lose only three to ten percent as heat. Indeed, the eerie glow is called "cold light."

When a female firefly waiting on the ground sees flashes of light at just the right time intervals and in a certain pattern, she turns on her light, a signal to the male of the same species that he has found a mate. The signals prevent wasting time during the rush to find a mate and breed.

Unique signals usually save time, but they occasionally bring an untimely death. The female of at least one species of firefly has perverted this language by mimicking the pattern of another type of firefly. When the male lands, he discovers not a waiting mate, but a hungry huntress.

Fireflies can afford to advertise their presence because they are unpalatable to many insect-eating animals. Indeed, some of these flying lanterns glow all the more brightly when handled roughly, suggesting that their glowing serves as a warning.

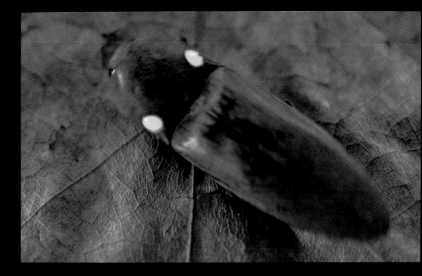

As he came near the Bahamas in 1492, Columbus witnessed the flamboyant spectacle of a group of bioluminescent marine animals. To him their lights looked like floating candles–to which fireworms, a bioluminescent worm common to that area, do indeed bear a marked resemblance when mating. Soon after a full moon, female fireworms leave their burrows in the seafloor and swim to the surface where they describe small circles, flashing their green lights off and on to give the go-ahead signal to the males. Seeing the lights, the males join the party to swim in an all-glowing fiery circle, as females lay eggs and males spread sperm.

In the peculiar looking deep-sea viperfish, dragonfish, and anglerfish, lights adorn either the end of a whiplike growth hanging from the chin or the tip of a "fishing pole" on top of the head. Glowing in the total darkness of the deep, these appendages lure other animals of the abyss. Seeking food, these unsuspecting victims become satisfying meals for the luminescent hunters.

Hunters never get everything their way, and though many fish of the dark depths use light to attract prey, some use light in a blinding defense. When one of them spots

Glowworms (opposite) illuminate the roof of a New Zealand cave that has become a tourist haunt. These larvae flash their lights to attract flying insects, which are caught in sticky strands when they come to investigate. Click beetles (above) shine tiny headlights. Brazilian Indians often caught them in perforated gourds for use as portable lamps.

Natural Lights

the light of another creature, it "flashes" its own lights suddenly, blinding the enemy much as a photographer's flash may blind his subject at close range. In the moments of the predator's staring stupor, the intended prey makes its getaway.

Light is used in another defensive way by certain squid inhabiting the middle levels of the Pacific Ocean. They light themselves up in order to hide. During the daytime, sunlight filters down through the water, and most animals appear as a silhouette to a hunter lurking below them. These squid turn on bluish lights along their lower surfaces to an intensity that matches the light filtering down through the sea. The color of their undersides then matches the water. In effect, the squid disappears. This trick requires not only organs that glow, but light-sensing organs that detect the level of light drifting down and monitor the light given off.

Bioluminescence is a double-edged sword. It can be used for repelling and attracting, for ending a life or for luring a mate to start life anew. Whatever their purpose, these living lights add an ethereal beauty to nature's gallery of amazing animals.

A sea pen (below), a type of coral, shimmers in the underwater darkness. Many sea pens glow when touched, sending ripples of light down the organism.

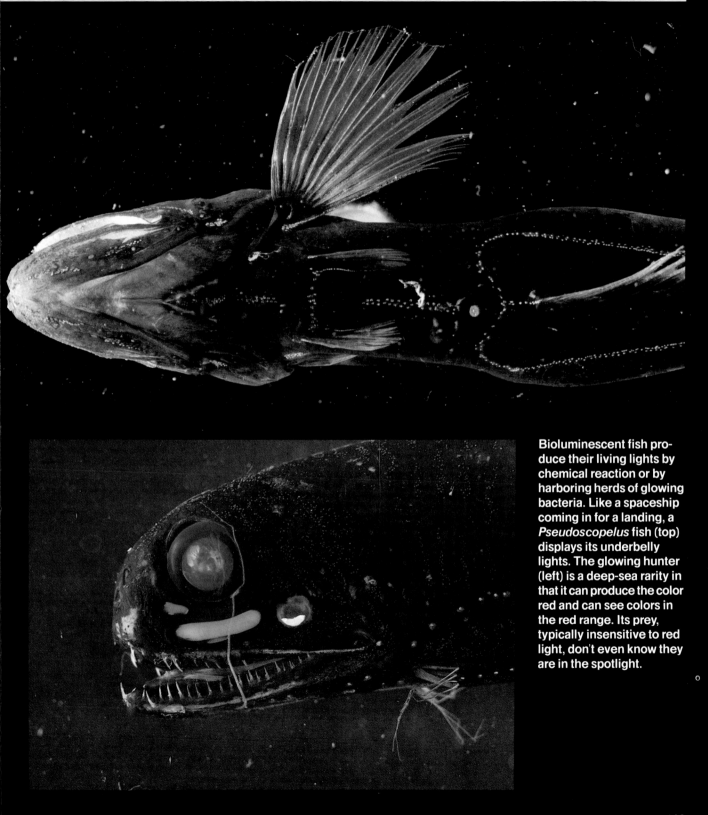

Bioluminescent fish produce their living lights by chemical reaction or by harboring herds of glowing bacteria. Like a spaceship coming in for a landing, a *Pseudoscopelus* fish (top) displays its underbelly lights. The glowing hunter (left) is a deep-sea rarity in that it can produce the color red and can see colors in the red range. Its prey, typically insensitive to red light, don't even know they are in the spotlight.

o

Late in the 18th century, a scientist discovered a remarkable talent in bats: Even with their vision blocked, they could fly through a maze of wires and not touch a strand. Plug their ears, though, and the bats hit the wires almost every time. This discovery was so extraordinary that scientists really didn't understand what it meant.

Today we know that bats, and some other creatures, use their hearing as part of a sonar system of navigation. They send out high-pitched clicks, often far higher than humans can hear. Then they listen for the echoes to help them locate obstacles and prey. We call this system, naturally enough, echolocation.

To get back echoes loud enough to hear, a bat must send out extra-strong clicks. Researchers have discovered that some bats really shout. Although we can't hear the clicks, their impact on the bat's eardrums is comparable to the blast of a jet engine on our ears. Such high volume presents a problem for the bat: how to keep from deafening itself. Fortunately, the bat's ears and brain take care of that.

In the middle ear, unusually well-developed muscles are attached to the bones that carry sound vibrations from the eardrum to the inner ear. When loud pulses are sent out, these muscles contract, damping the vibration of the bones and quieting the sound the bat hears. They quickly relax, though, so they don't interfere with the incoming echo. The brain itself is also designed to be especially sensitive to echoes: It responds more strongly to the second pulse of a given tone than to the first. Thus the first signal received, the bat's own click, will be only faintly perceived compared to the second signal, the echo.

Around the time that bat sonar was discovered, explorers in South America found another creature that had the peculiar ability to find its way around in pitch blackness: the cave-dwelling oilbird, also known as

guacharo, "one who cries and laments." Indeed, a colony of oilbirds disturbed in its dark cave sets up an incredible racket, once compared to the sound of "the last of the bathwater going down a particularly noisy drain." Through the din of the flying, squawking birds comes another sound, a clearly audible clicking. Though cruder than bats' ultrasonic beeps, these clicks provide the oilbirds with signals for echolocation.

At first, oilbirds might not seem to need sonar. They have excellent night vision, certainly adequate for finding their midnight snacks of palm and laurel fruits. In fact, outside their caves, they depend entirely on vision and smell. It is only in their subterranean homes that they rely on echoes to navigate the darkened passageways and to find their nests and waiting young. With echolocation, the oilbirds exploit the safety of the deep caves, never reached by the light of day or by sight-dependent wild predators.

Just as creatures of the air use echoes to find their way in darkness, other animals use echolocation for navigating the sunless depths of the sea. Cetaceans such as dolphins, porpoises, and killer whales send out a barrage of ultrasonic clicks, up to 1,000 a second. With them, they scan their surroundings and locate their food. Many whales also make lower-pitched sounds audible to humans, but they use these to communicate rather than navigate.

Just how whales make their sounds is still controversial since they have no vocal cords. Some researchers say that sudden movements of air back and forth in the nasal passages create the sounds, which are then projected forward through the tissue of the head.

The tissue in the front of the head forms a fatty body called the "melon." Its function is still a topic of hot debate, but many scientists believe that it focuses the animal's outgoing signals.

Detecting incoming signals is another

A pipistrelle bat (right, above) proves a formidable flying hunter. Locating insects with its sonar, one such bat caught one-fourth its weight in prey in barely half an hour. The oilbird (right, below) finds its nightly meal of fruit using keen vision enhanced by a reflecting eye layer that shines red in the photographer's flash. The bird uses its sonar for navigating through the dark caves where it lives.

BEYOND WILD EXPECTATIONS

Holding On

with the force of the waves with an added feature: a flexible "neck." Its shell covers only a portion of its head; the remainder, attached to the rock, is a tough, slender stalk resembling a goose's neck. When waves break over it, the gooseneck barnacle sways with the water like a willow bending in the wind without breaking.

Mussels also operate on the "bend without breaking" principle. To anchor itself to the rocks around it, a mussel secretes a sticky liquid from a gland near its foot. On contact with water or air, the liquid hardens into threads with attachment discs at their ends. The threads fan out from the mussel like a skirt of tiny anchors and are flexible enough to withstand the strain of a wave no matter where it pulls or pushes. The mussel rides the tide like a boat at anchor.

Other creatures take a different approach to withstanding the water's force. Shaped like a tiny volcano, the one-shelled limpet lets the full force of the waves press it ever more firmly against the rock. If it settles on hard rock, the limpet grinds the edge of its shell to fit the rock exactly; if the rock is soft enough, the limpet gouges a ring-shaped groove into which it fits its shell. Its muscular foot acts like a suction cup and the sloping shell shrugs off the force of the sea.

Chitons dissipate the power of the crashing waves by holding fast and maintaining a low profile. Their undersurface is a leathery girdle that conforms to any rock surface, and their backs are covered with eight flat plates. Chitons hold so tightly to their rocks that unless taken utterly by surprise they cannot be pried loose. This perseverance has enabled them to become one of the oldest surviving mollusks, pioneers of the sea's tempestuous edge.

With cement, sticky strands, and suction, these creatures of the intertidal zone survive in their hostile home. Their tenacity pays off. For the sea, along with its violence, brings doses of life-supporting water with roaring regularity. This larder is more than ample reward for holding on.

Rushing water washes over clinging starfish (opposite). Unable to survive long in air, the starfish follow the receding water as the tide falls. Mussels (left) anchor themselves to rocks or other mussels with tough threads. They survive the motion of the surf and waves like boats loosely held by mooring lines. A chiton (below and in the center of the photo) conforms to the shape of the rock with its leathery girdle. The flat contour of its back shrugs off the force of breaking waves.

BEYOND WILD EXPECTATIONS

Suntan Lotion

An animal's outer covering is no unimportant matter. Colorful feathers on birds and florid skin on mammals tantalize mates and intimidate competitors. Mottled hues, changeable colors, and even bold stripes conceal predator and prey alike. Fur keeps warmth in and cold out. Feathers mesh to shape wings, and skin stretches into flaps for gliding. But that's not all. The skin of animals living in sunny climates protects them from an ever-present danger—sunburn.

As every summertime vacationer knows, sun rays can cause painful burns. Lions, wildebeests, and other furred animals living under the hot sun are protected from burnt skin by their fur. The giraffe's tongue, exposed to the sun for hours as it plucks nourishing leaves, is a protective black. Living as they do over the shadeless sea and on barren island coasts, terns also have dark pigment to screen out burning rays. The noddy tern has black feathers; the fairy tern, translucent white ones—but black skin.

If an animal's skin appears naked before the full gaze of the sun, the animal probably has recourse to less obvious forms of protection than fur or color. Going about one's business at night is a sure way to avoid sunburn. The hippopotamus, for example, spends many nights on land browsing for grasses. There's no apparent reason for its eating at night, other than to escape the sun. This immense beast has nothing to fear from daytime predators.

The hippo spends its days up to its ears in Africa's rivers and mud flats, probably to avoid overheating in the sun. Its two-inch thick, hairless skin is less watertight than a person's. Perhaps it absorbs water, which then evaporates and cools the hippo. But parts of a wading hippo, especially its head, remain exposed to the sun. Exposed, yes, but not unprotected.

Glands in the hippo's skin bathe the flesh with a pink fluid that filters out the sun's burning rays. Observers used to think the animals sweated blood. Now we know that hippos exude their own suntan lotion. When painted on human skin, this fluid prevents both burning and tanning. Ah, wouldn't it be wonderful never to have to worry about burns and blisters after too much sun.

Hippos cooling off in a river are safely protected from the scorching sun. A pink fluid secreted by skin glands filters out the sun's ultraviolet rays.

The camel's exceptional endurance in the desert has been the source of popular misconceptions about the sturdy beast for centuries. It is commonly thought, for example, that the camel has an extra stomach for holding water. And many a schoolchild wrongly believes that the camel stores water in its huge hump.

The camel has, in fact, no separate water container at all. Its hump stores fat, not fluid. A camel can drink amazing amounts of water at a single time—up to 27 gallons in ten minutes—but manages to expend very little of that water between refills. In lands where moisture is at a premium, camels and other indigenous creatures survive because they excel as water hoarders.

The camel is adept at scrounging every possible bit of moisture from its environment—and at preserving all it can of its hard-earned supply. Its great nose, which contains a maze of passages lined with absorbent tissue, traps and soaks up moisture contained in the animal's breath. When the camel breathes in, warm, dry air passing through the moist nasal passages evaporates the moisture, cooling the nose and the air passing through it. When the animal

Although much mystique surrounds the camel's ability to live on little water, one of the secrets to this power is as plain as the nose on its face. Channels inside the nose absorb water vapor as the camel exhales, helping the desert animal conserve every available drop.

195

BEYOND WILD EXPECTATIONS

The Rain Makers

breathes out, the moisture in the breath condenses on, and is immediately reabsorbed by, the cooled nasal passages. The nose is then ready to cool the next intake of hot, dry air so that it doesn't heat the body. And since cool air holds less water than warm air, the camel's cooled breath carries out less water than it otherwise would.

While the amount of water retained this way may seem inconsequential, it makes a crucial difference over time. The camel's specialized nose reduces loss of water vapor by two-thirds what it is for mammals lacking comparable nasal architecture. Not surprisingly, other desert animals have noses that do the same thing. The tiny kangaroo rat recaptures as much as 88 percent of the moisture held in its breath.

Desert dwellers have other water-conservation techniques. The kangaroo rat produces urine so concentrated that it almost instantly solidifies when exposed to air. The camel, too, excretes urine and feces low in water. But in any desert mammal, the most significant threat to its internal water supply is loss through evaporation—from sweating and panting to cool off.

The kangaroo rat loses no fluid as sweat because, quite simply, it has no sweat glands. To control its temperature, it must remain in cool burrows most of the day. Camels do perspire, but they rely on the cool of night and on an amazing tolerance for fluctuations in body temperature to preserve fluid. The animal's temperature drops to a low of 93 degrees at night, then only gradually builds up during the day. A camel begins to sweat only when its temperature exceeds 105 degrees, thereby reducing the amount of water lost by sweating.

But when, in spite of all this, dehydration does occur, the camel is well prepared to cope with it. If a person in the heat of the desert loses water equal to 12 percent of his weight, he dies; a camel can lose over 22 percent of its body weight and survive. The dehydrated person is endangered because much of the water he loses comes from his blood. The thickened blood circulates less rapidly and, therefore, is less efficient in removing heat from inside the body. Heat builds up and death quickly follows. Even when the camel has lost more than a third of its body water, the water content of its blood remains largely stable; the camel loses water mostly from its tissues. Though weakened and emaciated by the dramatic loss, the camel copes. And a good, hearty drink restores it to a normal state in minutes.

No potential source of moisture goes untapped in the camel. It even has grooves that run from each nostril to its cleft upper lip so that any stray liquid from the nose finds its way to the camel's mouth.

Another desert creature is built to exploit similar grooves to an extraordinary degree. The spiny moloch lizard of Australia has skin covered with a network of microscopic canals. The moisture that reaches its skin travels along the grooves to the creature's mouth, where it is swallowed. In those parts of the planet where precious water is a scarce commodity, the secret of survival involves "keeping it to oneself."

Rugged animals inhabit rugged terrain. The creatures of the ever-parched desert must be their own rain makers. The camel (opposite) and the moloch lizard (below) are experts at making do with little water. The camel, for example, doesn't perspire until its temperature reaches 105 degrees. A network of tiny canals that fan over the lizard's skin collect any available moisture. The canals carry the droplets to the animal's mouth where they are swallowed.

BEYOND WILD EXPECTATIONS

Cooling Off

A fennec fox (opposite) stalks the African deserts. Its large ears allow it to maintain its body temperature by radiating excess heat. A waved albatross (above) lets off excess heat through its uninsulated legs that are cooled by the shade of its body.

As every athlete knows, panting and sweating cool an overheated body. Many animals cool off in this way, but some enhance the efficiency of this method in ingenious ways. Others, unable to sweat or pant, have less familiar but equally effective ways of keeping their cool.

Take the case of the rat-kangaroo, a marsupial. This nocturnal animal has a low metabolic rate. It burns fuel slowly and so generates low levels of body heat. When the animal becomes too warm, it pants to keep its temperature down. But if its temperature continues to climb, the animal's naked tail gets into the act; it begins to sweat profusely. To speed evaporation, the animal swings the wet tail from side to side.

Birds have no sweat glands, but they still must reduce excess body heat, even in cool air. Their high metabolism and characteristic activity—flying—generate tremendous internal heat. For example, a pigeon flying at 43 miles an hour produces 27 times the heat it does when at rest. How does it handle the buildup?

A bird usually releases heat through normal breathing, but when heat accumulates, the bird pants. Many birds also flutter their throat skin; this speeds up evaporation of moisture in the throat, speeding the cooling process. Standing in shade or cool water helps, too. Some birds urinate on their legs, which has the same cooling effect as sweating. And a number of birds, in particular the larger ones like turkey vultures and marabou storks, cope with the heat by spreading wide their wings. That, of course, increases the bird's exposed surface, allowing body heat to dissipate from a greater area.

The greater the surface area exposed to the air, the better an animal is able to dissipate heat. For this reason, small animals are better able to radiate heat than larger ones because they have more surface area in proportion to their body size. But animals are able to turn any ratio to their benefit if, like the large birds, they can increase their surface area when they are hot.

When people try to cool off by holding their arms out from their bodies in the heat, they increase their surface area. The fruit bat uses the same sort of air conditioning. It normally hangs upside down during the day, cloaked in its wings. But when it gets hot, it holds out its wings to cool itself.

Other animals have special features on their bodies to dissipate body heat. The ears of the fennec fox—like those of another desert-dweller, the jack rabbit—have large surface areas that emit excess heat. The foot-tall fennec fox has ears that grow to be six inches long and are densely packed

BEYOND WILD EXPECTATIONS

Cooling Off

with blood vessels that radiate heat.

An elephant's large ears also dissipate heat to keep the beast cool. When water is available, the elephant wets its ears and the rest of its body so that evaporation further lowers its temperature. The elephant's size also helps to protect it from heat. Although its enormous body is not as efficient as a smaller animal's in radiating heat, the heat from the sun simply takes a long time to permeate the massive bulk.

Not all animals shun heat. Like other cold-blooded animals, lizards need to absorb heat from the environment to warm themselves. But as with other animals, lizards die if they become overheated. To regulate their temperatures, they carefully select their surroundings. If they become too hot, for example, they move into shade. Several species of lizards are able to fine tune the amount of heat they take in by changing color. If they are cool and sluggish, their skin darkens to absorb heat. But if the body temperature of these dark-skinned lizards becomes dangerously high, their skin turns pale to reduce the amount of heat they absorb.

While creatures steal heat from the environment, they also use their surroundings to take heat away. Animals that wallow in mud have a messy but valuable means of cooling off. An experiment on pigs proved that a layer of mud is about eight times as effective as a douse in clear water for keeping the pigs cool: Mud enhances the cooling effect of water by holding more of it next to the skin. That partially explains why hippos and elephants and other animals of hot climates enjoy a good visit to a mudhole.

For man, who has long yearned to turn things ordinary into things of great value — say, straw into gold — there is much to admire in the ways elephants and hippos have of using mud and water to cope with the heat. But the mechanisms for coping are themselves astonishing. By adapting to the variety of earth's environments, each species takes a fascinating and very particular place among earth's amazing animals.

Fanning its ears wide in the blazing African sun, an elephant dissipates body heat through their large surface. Water evaporating from its skin enhances this natural air conditioning. The animal's size, though, is its most effective defense against the sun's rays. Its body is so huge, heat penetrates it slowly.

INDEX

CREDITS

Cover: M. P. Kahl **Page 1:** Tom Brakefield/Bruce Coleman, Inc. **2-3:** Bill McRae. **4-5:** R. Andrew Odum/Peter Arnold, Inc. **6:** Charles G. Summers, Jr.

WONDERS IN MOTION

Pages 8-9: John Dominis/Life Magazine © 1967 Time Inc. **10:** John Dominis/Life Magazine © 1967 Time Inc. **11:** Mohamed Amin/Bruce Coleman, Inc. **12:** Bob & Clara Calhoun/Bruce Coleman, Inc. **13:** Ron Austing. **15:** M. D. England/Ardea London. **16:** Stephen Dalton/NHPA. **18-19:** M. K. & I. M. Morcombe. **20:** Cliff B. Frith/Bruce Coleman, Inc. **21:** Cliff B. Frith/Bruce Coleman, Inc. **22-23:** G. L. Kooyman/Animals Animals. **24:** Oxford Scientific Films/Animals Animals. **25:** Runk/Schoenberger/Grant Heilman. **26:** James H. Carmichael, Jr. **27:** Carl Roessler. **28:** Peter David/Photo Researchers. **29:** Douglas Faulkner/Sally Faulkner Collection. **30 Top:** Keith Gillett/Tom Stack & Associates; **bottom:** D. P. Wilson/Eric & David Hosking. **31:** Zig Leszczynski/Animals Animals. **32:** Robert Noonan. **33:** Tom Myers. **34:** Zig Leszczynski/Animals Animals. **35:** Gary Milburn/Tom Stack & Associates. **36 Top:** James H. Carmichael, Jr.; **bottom:** Lois Cox. **37:** John Shaw. **38-39:** Fred Bruemmer. **40 Top:** Douglas Faulkner/Sally Faulkner Collection; **center:** Jack Drafahl/Image Concepts; **bottom:** Jack Drafahl/Image Concepts. **41:** Dale & M. Zimmerman/Bruce Coleman, Inc. **42:** Tom & Pat Leeson. **43 Top:** Erwin & Peggy Bauer; **bottom:** © Zoological Society of San Diego. **45:** Robert E. Pelham. **46-47:** Joe McDonald/

Bruce Coleman, Inc. **48:** Jack Dermid. **49 Top:** Tom McHugh/Photo Researchers; **bottom:** Courtesy of the American Museum of Natural History. **50:** Robert Noonan. **51 Top:** Thase Daniel; **bottom:** Ralph Morse/Life Magazine © 1969 Time Inc.

FEEDING THE BODY

Pages 52-53: Lynn Rogers. **54:** J. C. Carton/Bruce Coleman, Inc. **55:** Laura Riley. **56 Top:** Stephen Dalton/Animals Animals; **bottom:** Belinda Wright. **57:** Rajesh Bedi. **58:** Russ Kinne/Photo Researchers. **59:** Tom McHugh/Photo Researchers. **60:** Patricia Caulfield/Animals Animals. **61:** © Zoological Society of San Diego. **62 Top:** Tom McHugh; **center:** © Zoological Society of San Diego; **bottom:** Tom McHugh. **63 Top:** Frank J. Staub; **bottom:** Tim Fitzharris. **64 Top:** Dr. Edward S. Ross; **bottom:** Peter & Stephen Maslowski/Photo Researchers. **65:** Al Giddings/Ocean Images, Inc. **66:** Tom Myers. **68:** James H. Carmichael, Jr. **69 Top:** D. A. Craig; **bottom:** James H. Carmichael, Jr. **70:** Flip Schulke/Black Star. **71:** Dr. Edward S. Ross. **73 Top & bottom:** Hans Pfletschinger/Peter Arnold, Inc. **74:** Michael Morcombe. **75:** Oxford Scientific Films/Animals Animals. **76:** Dr. E. R. Degginger. **77:** John Tveten. **78 Top:** Fiona Sunquist/Tom Stack & Associates; **bottom:** Anthony & Elizabeth Bomford/Ardea London. **79 Top & bottom:** Jane Burton/Bruce Coleman, Inc. **80:** Tom McHugh. **81:** Stephen Dalton/Animals Animals. **82:** Alan Blank/Bruce Coleman, Inc. **83 Top & bottom:** Robert J. Shallenberger. **84 Top & bottom:** Robert J. Shallenberger. **85:** Stanley Breeden. **86-87:** Hans Reinhard/Bruce Coleman, Inc. **89:** Laura Riley. **90:** Annie Griffiths/Brandenburg Griffiths Photography. **91:** Francisco Erize/Bruce Coleman, Inc. **92:**

Fran Allan/Animals Animals. **93:** Tom Nebbia.

STAYING ALIVE

Pages 94-95: Norman Myers/Bruce Coleman, Inc. **96:** Alice B. Kessler. **97:** James H. Carmichael, Jr. **98 Top:** Jeff Foott/Bruce Coleman, Inc.; **bottom:** Kent & Donna Dannen. **99 Top:** Ben Cropp/Tom Stack & Associates; **bottom:** Allan Power/Bruce Coleman, Inc. **100:** Ed Degginger/Bruce Coleman, Inc. **101:** Dr. E. R. Degginger. **102 Top:** Edward S. Ross; **bottom:** Abe Blank/Bruce Coleman, Inc. **103:** P. Ward/Bruce Coleman, Inc. **104:** Lynn M. Stone. **105:** Robert Dunne. **106:** George B. Schaller/Bruce Coleman, Inc. **107 Top & bottom:** George B. Schaller/Bruce Coleman, Inc. **108 Top:** Tom McHugh/Photo Researchers, Inc.; **bottom:** Fred Bavendam/Peter Arnold, Inc. **109:** Zig Leszczynski/Animals Animals. **110:** Oxford Scientific Films/Animals Animals. **111:** Joe McDonald/Bruce Coleman, Inc. **112 Top:** Densey Clyne/Mantis Wildlife Films; **bottom:** William H. Amos. **113:** David Hosking/Eric & David Hosking. **114-115:** Tom Nebbia/DPI. **116:** Dr. E. R. Degginger. **117:** John MacGregor. **118 Top:** Jack Drafahl/Image Concepts; **bottom:** Jeffrey L. Rotman. **119:** James H. Robinson. **120 Top:** Kjell Sandved; **bottom:** Hans Pfletschinger/Peter Arnold, Inc. **122 Top:** Densey Clyne/Mantis Wildlife Films; **bottom:** Laura Riley/Bruce Coleman, Inc. **123:** Fritz Prenzel/Bruce Coleman, Inc. **124:** Douglas Faulkner/Sally Faulkner Collection. **125:** Dr. E. R. Degginger. **126:** Carl Roessler/Animals Animals. **127 Top:** John Boland; **bottom:** Edward S. Ross. **128:** Howard Hall/Tom Stack & Associates. **129:** James H. Carmichael, Jr./Bruce Coleman, Inc. **130:** Kjell Sandved. **131:** Anthony Bannister.

POPULATING THE FUTURE

Pages 132-133: Edward S. Ross. 134: Michael K. Morcombe. 135: Lynn L. Rogers. 136-137: Frans Lanting. 138: John Stern/Animals Animals. 139 Top: Jeff Foott; bottom: Dr. Edward S. Ross. 140 Top: Dr. Edward S. Ross; bottom: Jack Dermid. 141: Jeff Foott. 143: Stephen J. Krasemann/DRK Photo. 144: George H. Harrison/ Grant Heilman Photography. 145: Robert L. Dunne. 146-147: Jen & Des Bartlett/Bruce Coleman, Inc. 148: B. G. Murray, Jr./ Animals Animals. 149 Top: Dwight R. Kuhn; bottom: Wiles F. Mitchell. 150 Top & bottom: Carl Roessler. 151: Richard C. Kern/James A. Kern. 152: Jen & Des Bartlett/Bruce Coleman, Inc. 153: Tom McHugh. 155: Erwin & Peggy Bauer. 156: Henry Genthe. 157: Photographic Library of Australia. 158: C. Allan Morgan. 159: C. Allan Morgan. 160: Phil Dotson/DPI. 161: Brian Milne. 162: Bob McKeever/Tom Stack & Associates. 163: Howard Hall/Tom Stack & Associates. 164: William J. Weber. 165: Martin W. Grosnick.

BEYOND WILD EXPECTATIONS

Pages 166-167: Steven C. Wilson/ Entheos. 168: Carleton Ray. 169: Lynn L. Rogers. 170-171: Jeff Foott. 171: Michael R. Stoklos/ Animals Animals. 172: © Zoological Society of San Diego. 173: Ivan Polonin/NHPA. 174-175: Kevin Schafer/Tom Stack & Associates. 176 Left: Kjell B. Sandved, Smithsonian Inst.; right: Constance P. Warner. 177: Jen & Des Bartlett/ Bruce Coleman, Inc. 178: Wolfgang Kaehler. 179 Top & bottom: Carleton Ray. 180: Brian Brake/Photo Researchers, Inc. 181: Oxford Scientific Films/ Bruce Coleman, Inc. 182: Jeffrey L. Rotman. 183 Top & bottom: Peter David/Seaphot Ltd. 185

Top: Hans Reinhard/Bruce Coleman, Inc.; bottom: Dr. Edward S. Ross. 186: Zig Leszczynski/ Animals Animals. 187: Dr. Edward S. Ross. 188: Steve Martin/Tom Stack & Associates. 189: Robert O. Schuster. 190-191: Mike Price/Bruce Coleman, Inc. 192: Jeff Foott. 193 Top: E. R. Degginger/Bruce Coleman, Inc.; bottom: Jeff Foott. 194: Bob Campbell/Bruce Coleman, Inc. 195: P. Forge/Explorer. 196: Giorgio Gualco/Bruce Coleman, Inc. 197: Jim Frazier/Mantis Wildlife Films. 198: Leonard Lee Rue III/Animals Animals. 199: George H. Harrison. 200-201: Tom Nebbia/DPI.

Some art in this book is based on art in the sources shown below.

Page 10: Milton Hildebrand, "How Animals Run," Scientific American, vol. 202, no. 5 (May, 1960), p. 152.

Page 17: Martin Wells, Lower Animals (New York: McGraw-Hill Book Company, 1968), p. 115, © Weidenfeld & Nicolson Publishing Co., Ltd.

Page 44 Left: Miriam Rothschild, et al., "The Flying Leap of the Flea," Scientific American, vol. 229, no. 5 (November, 1973), p. 93.

Page 45: Rainer F. Felix, Biology of Spiders (Cambridge, MA: Harvard University Press, 1982), p. 155. Taken from photographs by Parry and Brown, Journal of Experimental Biology, vol. 36 (1959), p. 654.

Page 51: Richard C. Snyder, "Bipedal Locomotion of the Lizard Basiliscus basiliscus," Copeia, 2 (June, 1949), p. 133.

Page 54: Bryan Nelson, The Gannet (South Dakota: Buteo Books, 1978), p. 221.

Page 58: Dr. Philip Whitfield, The Hunters (New York: Simon and Schuster, 1978), p. 29, © Marshall Editions Ltd.

Page 70: Whitfield, p. 41, and Paul A. Meglitsch, Invertebrate

Zoology (New York: Oxford University Press, 1967), p. 134.

Page 78: W. C. Osman Hill, Primates, Comparative Anatomy and Taxonomy (New York: Interscience Publishers, Inc., 1953), p. 669. Distributed by Columbia University Press. © Edinburg University Press.

Page 80: Eric A. Newman and Peter H. Hartline, "The Infrared Vision of Snakes," Scientific American, vol. 246, no. 3 (March, 1982), p. 119.

Page 88: Adapted from an illustration by Robert Gillmor. John Sparks and Tony Soper, Owls, Their Natural and Unnatural History (New York: Taplinger Publishing Co., Inc., 1970), p. 20. By permission.

Page 101: Michael and Patricia Fogden, Animals and their Colors (New York: Crown Publishers, Inc., 1974), p. 29, © Eurobook Ltd.

Page 111: Adapted from an illustration by Robert Gillmor. John Sparks and Tony Soper, Owls, Their Natural and Unnatural History (New York: Taplinger Publishing Co., Inc., 1970), p. 15. By permission.

Page 121: Kenneth D. Roeder, "Moths and Ultrasound," Scientific American, vol. 212, no. 4 (April, 1965), p. 102.

Page 141: John K. Terres, The Audubon Society Encyclopedia of North American Birds (New York: Alfred A. Knopf, 1980), p. 474, illustration © Margaret LaFarge.

Page 149: Werner Nachtigall, Insects in Flight (New York: McGraw-Hill Book Company, 1968), p. 143, © George Allen & Unwin Ltd.

Page 152: Illustration based on photograph by Marineland of Florida.

Page 156: Illustration based on photograph by Henry Genthe.

Page 188: E. C. Migdalski and G. S. Fichter, The Fresh and Salt Water Fishes of the World (New York: Alfred A. Knopf, 1976), p. 88, © Vineyard Books, Inc.

Library of Congress Cataloging in Publication Data

Main entry under title:

Earth's amazing animals.

Includes index.
1. Zoology.
I. National Wildlife Federation.
QL50.E24   1983   591   83-17324
ISBN 0-912186-48-8

National Wildlife Federation

1412 16th Street, N.W.
Washington, D.C. 20036

Dr. Jay D. Hair
Executive Vice President

James D. Davis
*Senior Vice President
Membership Development
and Publications*

Staff for this Book

Howard F. Robinson
Managing Editor

Cecilia I. Parker
Editor

Donna Miller
Design Director

Polly S. White
Art Editor

Laura B. Ackerman
Research Editor

Vi Kirksey
Donna Reynolds
Editorial Assistants

Priscilla Sharpless
Production and Printing

Margaret E. Wolf
Permissions Editor

Pam McCoy
Dolores Motichka
Production Artists

Victor H. Waldrop
Michael E. Loomis
Editorial Contributors

Thomas B. Allen
Karen Jensen
Philip Kopper
Writers

Biruta Akerbergs
Illustrator

Dr. Bruce Beehler
Secretary's Research Lab

Dr. John Cadle
Division of Herpetology

Dr. Charles Crumly
Division of Herpetology

Dr. Charles O. Handley, Jr.
Division of Mammals

Mr. Gary F. Hevel
Department of Entomology
    National Museum of Natural
    History, Smithsonian
    Institution

Dr. George A. Middendorf, III
Department of Zoology
    Howard University

Mr. Craig Phillips
Fish and Wildlife Service,
    U.S. Department of the Interior

Scientific Consultants